Coaching the Air Raid Offense is the best football book I have read in years. Coach Hargitt has given readers an amazing resource on the most popular attack in offensive football. This well-organized material can be utilized from the junior high level all the way up through the NFL.

Scott E. Peach
Head Football Coach
Arlington (TX) High School

Coach Hargitt has done a great job of breaking down the air raid offense. He is a good student of the game. I enjoyed his book and gained some valuable information about the air raid offense.

Del Van Cox
Offensive Coordinator
Abilene (TX) High School

Coaching the Air Raid Offense is as complete a reference to a spread offense as I have seen. It is very organized and easily understood—it was like I was standing there talking to Coach Hargitt about each part of the book as I read it!

Chris Andriano
Head Football Coach
Montini Catholic High School (IL)

Coaching the Air Raid Offense is very thorough in explaining all aspects of the air raid system. Organized in a way that makes it easy to follow, the book includes particular information about everything coaches need to know to run the scheme.

Strait Herron
Head Football Coach
South Pointe High School (SC)

The thing that sets Coach Hargitt's work apart from others is his attention to detail. In this book, he outlines every aspect of the air raid offense. It is the most complete ready reference on this explosive offense that I've come across.

Lew Johnston
Head Football Coach
Nansemond-Suffolk Academy (VA)

Coaching the Air Raid Offense

Rich Hargitt

©2014 Coaches Choice. All rights reserved. Printed in the United States.

No part of this book may be reproduced, stored in a retrieval system, or transmitted, in any form or by any means, electronic, mechanical, photocopying, recording, or otherwise, without the prior permission of Coaches Choice. Throughout this book, the masculine shall be deemed to include the feminine and vice versa.

ISBN: 978-1-60679-282-7
Library of Congress Control Number: 2013948001
Cover design: Cheery Sugabo
Book layout: Studio J Art & Design
Front cover photo: Getty Images
Front cover background: iStockphoto/Thinkstock
Back cover author photo: Jim Hargitt
Text photos: Lisa Hargitt

Coaches Choice
P.O. Box 1828
Monterey, CA 93942
www.coacheschoice.com

Dedication

This work is dedicated to my wonderful wife, Lisa, and our handsome sons, Griffin and Graham. Thanks to my wife for all the endless support in coaching and to my sons for showing me what is really important in this life. Finally, this work is dedicated above all to God, who gives me the ability to live each day with strength and honor.

Acknowledgments

I would like to thank my beautiful wife, Lisa, and our sons, Griffin and Graham, who support me. Thanks also to my parents who gave me the foundation to be a successful coach.

I would like to thank a wide variety of coaches who have helped me learn a great deal about the spread offense in general—and the air raid version of it in particular. First, I would like to thank the father of the air raid offense, Hal Mumme, who has offered unquestionably good insight into the offense that he has helped to pioneer. I would also like to thank Matt Mumme, the offensive coordinator at Davidson College in Davidson, North Carolina, Marc Kolb the offensive coordinator at Tusculum College in Greenville, Tennessee, Stan Zweifel and Jake Olsen of the University of Dubuque, and Dale Carlson, the head football coach at Valparaiso University in Valparaiso, Indiana.

Fellow high schools coaches have helped in numerous ways to provide me with insight into various aspects of the spread offense and the air raid offense. These generous coaches include: Brent Eckley of Jackson High School (MO), Matt Beam of Burns High School (NC), Lee Sadler of Mountain Home High School (AR), John Allison and Ken Leonard of Sacred Heart-Griffin High School (IL), Derek Leonard of Rochester High School (IL), Mark Grounds of Jacksonville High School (IL), Brian Hales of Butler High School (NC), Bob Gaddis of Columbus East High School (IN), Lance Sheib of Noblesville High School (IN), and Kevin Wright of Carmel High School (IN). Thanks also to Rex Lardner for helping me get exposure for this offense, and to the great people at Coaches Choice, especially Kristi Huelsing, who did so much to help me with this project. Thanks also to Aaron Coughlin and the great people at the Glazier Clinics for helping me get the opportunity to speak on this offense and gain exposure for it nationally.

I would also like to give thanks to Coach Dave Farquharson for always being there to bounce ideas off of and traveling the country to learn more football. Secondly, thanks to Randy Niekamp for all the time on the phone and in person, and for being such a source of information and support.

Finally, I would like to acknowledge the athletes in Illinois, Indiana, North Carolina, and South Carolina who ran our system and worked so hard to represent their faith, family, and football program with such class.

Foreword

When Rich Hargitt asked me to write the foreword for his new book, I accepted his request based on my recent correspondence with him. I was honored to do this because I think Rich Hargitt is one of the brightest young coaches that I have met in some time. It is rare to find a 32-year-old coach who has the knowledge, expertise, and passion for the game of football that Rich embodies. I am entering my 27th year as a high school head football coach, and during that time I have witnessed many offensive systems. The challenge we coaches have today is to stay current and informed. Offensive football has exploded with new concepts. Coaches who are content to stay with the old systems will get left behind very quickly.

In the early 1980s, I was the offensive coordinator for a small Division II college. The I formation and full-house wishbone were the hot offenses at that time. Coaches who changed to these systems in the mid to late 1970s were coming from systems of single-wing, wing-T, or the Notre Dame box. These were system offenses that gave an order to football in terms of structure, game planning, and play call. Coaches who were trained in these systems were comfortable with the game management and the answers that these systems provided. Many of these systems are still utilized today with success; however, installation of these systems requires techniques that are considered antiquated to the current game. I personally utilized the wing-T offense with a triple option blend. This offense was instrumental in taking our football teams to several playoff appearances, four semi-final games, and a state championship in the early 1990s. Defenses caught up with our system, creating more and more issues moving the ball. We could still beat the bad or average teams, but our reputation of beating great teams with our lesser talent was no longer the case. I bounced around with different offensive systems to find some answers, but only recently after meeting with Rich Hargitt do I feel that we are on track.

As coaches, we are always looking for creative ways to give less talented offensive personnel a chance to compete against superior defensive talent. Modern defenses now understand the old systems of two and three running backs, making it difficult to win consistently in those systems. I am not saying that you cannot win with those systems today. You can, but the teams that win big in those systems usually have superior personnel and feeder systems in place to develop them.

The spread offense is now the offense of choice in many programs around the country. In my search to learn more about spread offense, I ran across a DVD package produced by Rich Hargitt and purchased it. The more I watched, the more I realized that his approach to teaching spread offense was unique and simple. I called his school that same day and worked out a visit for our coaching staff. That visit to meet with Coach Hargitt was very informative and worthwhile. He gave us a clear understanding about attacking different types of secondary coverage. He showed us how to use the screen game effectively. His teaching progression and communication for the no-huddle offense was most beneficial. He also gave us answers to problem defenses and basically got an "old coach" to see a systematic order to spread offense that I had never considered. It also became clear that many of the old run systems (wing-T, single wing, etc.) are great for the running game in spread formations. Rich explained that you still put defenders in conflict; the point of attack has simply moved out from the core of the defense to the perimeter. Once I grasped that concept, I was able to move forward in planning the scope of our offense.

Now you have all of this information in his new book. I would recommend that any coach should have a copy of this book for a resource. If you will follow Coach Hargitt's principles, you will find—as we did—that this system is very well thought out and solid.

Mike Earwood
Head Football Coach
Our Lady of Mercy Catholic High School (GA)

Contents

Dedication 5

Acknowledgments 6

Foreword 7

Preface 10

Introduction 12

Chapter 1: Air Raid Philosophy 15

Chapter 2: Air Raid Personnel 18

Chapter 3: Practice Plan 24

Chapter 4: Formations 34

Chapter 5: No-Huddle Communication—Formations 44

Chapter 6: No-Huddle Communication—Plays 52

Chapter 7: Run Plays 59

Chapter 8: Screen Plays 68

Chapter 9: Air Raid Quick Passing Game 77

Chapter 10: Air Raid Dropback Passing Game 89

Chapter 11: Air Raid Game Planning 106

Conclusion 117

About the Author 119

Preface

The air raid offense has been a part of the college football landscape for quite some time. It is enjoying success at the collegiate and high school level each fall and making defensive coordinators prepare for its fast pace and lightning-quick scoring potential. The journey really began with the work that LaVell Edwards put in at BYU in making the forward pass a legitimate weapon on the college football field. The trend has continued, and a quick look at what teams like Baylor University, Texas Tech University, West Virginia University, Oklahoma State University, and Texas A&M University are doing will convince even the passing observer that the air raid is alive and well today. Several years ago, my staff and I were looking for a way to revolutionize the style of offense we played. We were trying to run the football and play traditional styles of offense, and we routinely found ourselves being physically dominated by athletically superior opponents. We learned about the air raid system and really came to believe that the idea of "throwing the ball quickly to people who can score" meant that a team could learn to compete against superior opponents by utilizing the forward pass.

The air raid offense was adopted in 2011 at Nation Ford High School (SC) and used to achieve the school's first playoff berth and first playoff victory that fall. In 2012, Nation Ford utilized the air raid offense to upset several ranked teams and produced school records in wins in a season (7), yards passing for a season (2,866), yards passing in a game (415), yards from scrimmage in a season (4,430), points scored in a season (357), and average points scored in a game (30). The air raid offense helped lead Nation Ford to a AAAA playoff berth and the school's first winning season. The air raid quarterbacks at Nation Ford High School have passed for 4,630 yards in the last two seasons, putting them near the top of every statistical category in their area.

The air raid has taken a high school that had no tradition and very low prospects of success, and in just two years transformed it into a winner. In addition, there is a constant interest from people around the country in what the team does offensively. The air raid system of offense makes things very fun to watch and even more fun to participate in each fall. It has allowed the school to not only compete against some of the best football teams in the Southeastern United States, but it has also built for them a reputation and something that they can hang their hat on that is unique and fun.

A great many coaches have interpreted the offense differently and put their own twists on it over the years. Some years, my teams have thrown the ball predominantly, and other years they have been a more ground-oriented team with the run game. The point behind the offense is two simple things, and these two things guide most of my thoughts. The first thing I look to do with the offense is attack defenses. The air raid allows a coach to put pressure on the entire width and depth of a football field with a variety of simple pass plays and base run plays. This ability to attack with diversity allows the offense to find the weak links in a defense and do the most damage. The second thing I look for is what I call the fun factor. I want the offense to be new, fun, and mentally engaging for the coaches, athletes, and fans. By running a system that is fun to play in and watch, I feel that a program can attract top-notch athletes and keep the fan base energized and supportive. Many distractions can keep young men from being involved in school-sponsored activities. When a football game is transformed into a fast-paced and fun-filled adventure by the way that the coaches teach and coach, then it is much easier to get young people attracted to the concept of playing the sport. The air raid offense has allowed my teams to do this and have a great deal of success along the way.

Introduction

Spread offenses are taking the organized football world by storm. The proliferation of multiple-receiver sets and high-scoring attacks have been coupled with the no-huddle and are currently wreaking havoc on the minds of defense coordinators from coast to coast. Offenses from every state in the union (and even some from as far away as Europe) are spreading out defenses and attacking them with almost surgical precision. The air raid offense contributed greatly to this new style of football that has even found its way into collegiate and professional ranks this fall. The modern era of football features spread formations, no-huddle tempo, and dazzling numbers of offensive production.

The air raid offense was pioneered by football mastermind Hal Mumme. Mumme worked at Iowa Wesleyan College with such football household names as Mike Leach and Dana Holgorsen. Mumme took the system to Valdosta State University, the University of Kentucky, and McMurray College, and he has continued to build prolific offenses year after year. The air raid family tree expanded out to include the likes of Tony Franklin, Sonny Dykes, Chris Hatcher, and Matt Mumme. The system has hooked many coaches by employing simple rules and concepts that allow the offense to get the ball to skill players in space. The majority of teams that employ the air raid offense do so because their athletes cannot line up in traditional offensive structures and win by running the football right at their opponents. The air raid allows the offense to dictate the style and pace of the game and create multiple 1-on-1 match-ups in the passing game that give the offense a chance to move the football and score points. The air raid is neither a complex system, nor one that requires exceptional athletes, but it literally helped to change the face of football forever.

The air raid offense is very much a concept-based offense. The idea of concepts means there are no route trees, and the players simply know what to do based upon the call from the sideline. If a concept is signaled in to the game, the athletes all know their assignments respective to where they are lined up in a given formation. Many air raid teams have added the use of the no-huddle tempo to their offensive arsenals. The principal method of no-huddle that most air raid teams have employed will be through the use of hand signals to play at an extremely fast tempo. The air raid pushes the defense to their physical and mental limits by attacking vertically and horizontally in the pass game, as well as bringing to bare a full complement of run and screen plays. The increased pace of the offense will require teams to be forced to defend this wide open offense at a tremendously quick pace in which the ball can be snapped every seven seconds. The natural pass-first mentality of the offense coupled with this increased pace has been causing defenses to restructure and retool themselves in ways that are making themselves more susceptible to being exploited by modern offenses.

The final aspect of the air raid offense that is essential to be understood is the quarterback's read progression. In the air raid, quarterbacks are coached to make a pre-snap read on the deepest route on the field. This initial read is commonly referred to as a "peek" or pre-snap read. The quarterback looks at any vertical deep route from a receiver and makes a decision before the ball is snapped if he wants to throw to this player. If the quarterback deems this a good possibility of a big offensive play, he throws the deep ball off his last step, but if this read is cloudy, he will work back into the progression. The quarterback's first read is the lowest or shallowest receiver in the pattern. This is done to create more quick throws that come out on rhythm and give the offense a higher completion percentage. The air raid's premise it that it will work the ball to receivers in space quickly and let them work with the ball in their hands. The aspect of throwing the ball to receivers quickly prevents negative plays by the quarterback and puts stress on the defense. The defense is constantly forced to rush the quarterback, but they are often unable to get to him. This adds to the fatigue and frustration factors for the defense. In addition, the offense is getting the ball to its best athletes in space and giving them a chance to make big plays. The quarterback's second read is to the middle or intermediate route in the pattern. For example, the Florida (or flood) play would be a peek to the outside receiver running the clear-out vertical, then the first read is to the flat runner, and the second read is to the bench or sail route. This progression allows the quarterback to always have a consistent feel for the game and to make quick decisions.

The air raid offense has shown that it is a great way to move the ball and score points in today's game. In order for this system to be successful, it is imperative that both coaches and players buy into the system. In an era when more and more athletes are lost to the idea of playing more "fun" things like basketball or other rec league types of sports, the air raid offense allows the football coach to recruit heavily from his own hallways by establishing a brand that athletes will buy into each season. The air raid offense is very fun to play in, so a wide variety of skill-type players will have fun in the system, and word will spread that it is something to be a part of each season. The major theme of the air raid offense is simply to find open grass and throw the ball to highly skilled players who can score. This system will excite young players and get them out for the team as well as hold them in the program for years by simply allowing them to touch the ball, score points, and have fun.

1

Air Raid Philosophy

The basic philosophy of the air raid offense when it was created was to "throw the ball short to people who can score." The offense has always prided itself on being a pass-first system of offense that develops a simple run game to complement an aerial assault. Many air raid teams will earn a reputation for being a pass-happy football team even though the truth is that they may run the ball up to 50 percent of the time. This reputation is earned because most air raid teams spend a great deal of their practice time throwing the ball and have inflicted a great deal of damage on opposing defenses with it. That statement reflects the most basic premise of why many teams employ the air raid offense: the ability to strike quickly. Many air raid teams, especially those at the high school level but even in the college ranks, are not able to line up play after play and attack the quality defenses they see week in and week out in a traditional pro set and hope to be successful. Therefore, it has become necessary to employ a system with which the offense can attack vulnerabilities in the defense without having to be athletically superior.

Most teams have at least a few good athletes who can win 1-on-1 match-ups. In the air raid offense, these athletes are often placed at receiver, and the system directs the ball to these athletes quickly. Quarterbacks are taught to read the field quickly and get the ball to these athletes before the defense can react. This philosophy ensures that the protection does not have to hold up long nor does the offense have to expect to block many defenders. The system is predicated on getting the ball to people who can score quickly and letting them make moves with the ball in their hands to create plays and advance the ball down the field.

A basic philosophical component of the air raid offense is to move quickly and not give teams a chance to adjust on defense to what the offense is attempting to do. The offense is not particularly complicated, nor is a massive amount of plays involved. The air raid is predicated on the offensive players learning a limited numbers of plays from a wide variety of formation structures. This allows the offense to look very multiple and give the defense a lot to process while keeping things simple to learn. In order for an air raid team to keep the defense guessing, it is necessary to play the game at an advanced tempo so that the defenders cannot attack the offensive package with new coverages or stunts. In addition, most air raid teams lack large and imposing linemen, especially at the high school level, and so the idea of reducing the time between plays appeals to the idea of fatiguing the defense by forcing them to play faster and adjust to multiple formations.

The no-huddle allows a team to get to the line of scrimmage quickly and make decisions that put the offense in an advantageous position. It also allows the offense to fatigue a defense that is often athletically superior to the offense. When traditional offenses come to the line and have a play called, they are at the mercy of defensive shifts, stunts, and blitzes. The air raid employs a fast paced tempo version of no-huddle that forces defenses to play very "vanilla" (or plain) in their defensive packages. These defensive structures then become easily identifiable and easier to assault. The tempo aspect of the offense then allows the play caller to know where the defense will align and call plays that allow his athletes to make the most out of a route or run block. This philosophy serves the offense well and is one that should be employed regardless of athletic ability. The tempo can he sped up or slowed down based upon what is needed by the offense at any given time. Motion is utilized when and where it is applicable to give the offense an increased advantage of numbers. Many times, motion will distort an already fatigued defense's thought process and create favorable numbers advantages for the offense.

The air raid is primarily a spread-based offense, and therefore the formations are standard in terms of 2x2, 3x1, 3x2, and other spread sets. However, over time the offense has expanded to include the use of one or two tight ends and also multiple backfield sets. A trend toward incorporating pistol formations in to the air raid to adapt to personnel needs has begun. The philosophy of coaches today in the air raid is to adapt these formations and utilize them to keep defenses off balance while maintaining the base integrity of the system. The common sense approach to no-huddle signals has allowed the air raid to adapt to whatever personnel and structural needs that coaches wish to implement. The proof of this is clearly seen when watching air raid–inspired teams such as the West Virginia Mountaineers or Oklahoma State Cowboys. These two programs are both spread-based air raid teams, but they are able and willing to use multiple formations and move their athletes into advantageous positions all while maintaining high tempo pace of movements.

The running game in this offense is kept very simple to allow the athletes and coaches to focus their time on refining the passing game. Therefore, the run game is based around the inside and outside zone principles. Recently, a gap scheme of power and counter plays have been utilized to give the offense more hitting power in short-yardage situations. Therefore, the athletes are only required to learn two blocking schemes (zone and gap), and only four total plays. This simplicity makes it possible to run more repetitions of each play and, therefore, become more proficient as a running team. While the air raid will never be a run-first system, many teams have become very good at running the ball because the system is so simple that it can be taught and performed by a wide range of athletes. In addition, a wide variety of quick and slow screens are often tied into these run plays to make them even more lethal toward the defense while keeping the base integrity of two blocking schemes to maintain simplicity.

The passing game is the primary basis of why a team would select the air raid as its primary method of offensive production. To that end, the quarterback is by far the most important position to consider when selecting the system. The quarterback needs to have at least an average arm and also at least average speed, but he must be an exceptional leader with a great deal of instinct for the game and a general desire to be a continuous student of the system. The reads are not particularly complicated in the air raid passing game, but the quarterback must be able to make accurate decisions under duress and replicate those decisions very quickly. Therefore, philosophically speaking, a quarterback must be selected that is very much an extension of the coaching staff. This young man must like the game and like sitting down to scheme and immerse himself mentally in the game for the team to be successful. The quarterback in this system will flourish because of his ability to make correct decision with speed and deliver the ball with accuracy and so the "big armed" quarterback that very few schools can actually find is not essential to run the system. In addition, because so much of the offense is predicated on quick throws from the shotgun, you will find several cases of shorter quarterbacks being successful in the air raid. Quarterbacks such as Case Keenum at Houston and Johnny Manziel at Texas A&M have lit up scoreboards using the air raid system despite the fact that they are many times framed as "undersized" by the media. The air raid allows a wide variety of quarterbacks to be successful, and so it is easier to recruit a quarterback for this system than more traditional offenses.

The air raid offense is a simple marriage of quickness of pace and aggressive play calling that makes defense adjust to it. The main objective when calling plays is to make defenses adjust to the offense and put pressure on all 11 defensive players to find weaknesses. The opportunities to line up and physically dominate people are very limited, so finding a corner who is poor in coverage or a defensive end who does not keep contain is paramount in being successful. The air raid is a pass-first system that is always attacking, always pushing the tempo, and always searching the field for ways to stretch defenders and put them into new and innovative conflicts that increase the likelihood of offensive success.

2

Air Raid Personnel

Coaches planning to use the air raid offense need to get the most out of each of the 11 positions on the offensive side of the ball. It is critical to ensure that each athlete is on the same page and has the same knowledge of what is expected on each play. When the entire offense is working together, the chance of scoring points will be greatly increased.

The air raid is most effective when the offense can take advantage of a weakness that the defense has shown. The quarterback, skilled players, and linemen need to be able to identify these weaknesses and exploit them on the field. Getting an athlete to understand the importance of finding open space, moving at a fast pace is critically important. In addition, always using the philosophy of mentally and physically moving on to the next play, regardless of the previous plays outcome, is a critical component in a successful air raid offense.

The key to taking advantage of the defense is to make sure to use a limited amount of substitutions. It is preferable to recruit and train versatile athletes who will allow a team to switch from formation to formation without allowing the defense to make adjustments. By keeping the same 11 athletes on the field, it will allow for a no-huddle offense, which keeps the defense guessing and off balance. It is then necessary to train athletes to play more than one position. For this reason, the Y-receiver position and the H-back position are often cross-trained hybrid athletes who can play multiple positions on the football field.

This chapter will help a coach identify the basic qualities and abilities that might be looked for in each of the 11 positions on the field. These traits are by no means all-inclusive, and different athletes have served the offense well over the years. Some years, a shorter athlete can play a position better than a taller athlete, or a heavy player maybe offers something that a lighter player does not. The point is not so much what the athlete looks like, but what he is capable of doing for the offense. By getting the most out of each of the athletes utilized, the air raid offense can be successful at any school or level.

Quarterback

The quarterback is the engine that makes the air raid offense successful. This position is where the best athlete on the team with the most overall football savvy must be placed. The quarterback must be extremely football smart. He will be responsible for knowing each route and blocking scheme. He must be able to identify defensive fronts and coverages by quickly scanning an opposing defense. By doing so, he will be able to make sure the offense is attacking the weakness of the defense. He needs to be able to communicate to the coaches and players what he is seeing during a time-out or change of possession with clear and concise communication. The quarterback needs to be confident in his abilities and not easily shaken. He needs to be able to put any play, regardless of good or bad outcome, behind him and move on to the next play. He needs to be an excellent decision-maker and make the correct reads and deliver the ball to his playmakers. In essence, this young man must be an extension of the coaching staff on the field. Many coaches talk about height, weight, arm strength, and other physical characteristics to describe a good quarterback. These traits are all important, but one thing that a life spent coaching football will teach a person is that quarterbacks come in all shapes, colors, and styles. The position requires mental acuity and a passion to excel that is supported more than initiated by peak physical abilities. The recruitment, selection, and coaching of the quarterback will influence the success of the air raid offense more than any other personnel decision made by a coach.

X-Receiver

This receiver should be the best receiver on a team. This athlete should be the fastest person on the offensive side of the ball and the athlete most able to defeat a single coverage defender. He needs to have the ability to take the top off of the defense. By doing so, he opens up the underneath for multiple crossing and mesh routes, and also helps the run game by pulling defenders out of the box. This player should be an above-average athlete who can win almost all 1-on-1 battles and force the defense to defend him anywhere on the field. He needs to be able to make the big play if a defense decides to give him the opportunity. This athlete's height and weight should not be overemphasized. He should be a dynamic football player who is not to be taken lightly and likes to work deep and attack coverages. He need not be the most football smart athlete on the team, but he should be one of the best physical specimens an offense can produce.

Z-Receiver

This player must be a good athlete, with a lot of football knowledge. He will be required to make plays both in the quick game and still be a vertical threat. He should have very good hands and be relied upon to make catches in traffic. He needs to be able to win 1-on-1 situations and take advantage of single coverage caused by the speed of the X-receiver. Often times, the Z-receiver is a great athlete who lacks the overall down-the-field speed to play the X-receiver position, or he is maybe not big or strong enough to handle a defense's best corner in coverage. The Z-receiver often gets more balls thrown to him because of his versatility. If this athlete is a good football player, then he makes the X-receiver better and vice versa.

Y-Receiver/Tight End

The Y-receiver is by far the most critical position on the field from a recruitment standpoint. If a tight end is in the offense, then this is the position he will play. Many teams have a hard time finding a good blocking tight end who can also catch passes, so they substitute two different athletes who can play the position. This is not an option in the air raid offense because of the refusal to substitute athletes. If this position has to be substituted, then it seriously hinders the ability to be a no-huddle team. Therefore, this position requires a great deal of time to cultivate. A suggestion would be: when trying to find this athlete, open the competition to the entire team. Many defensive ends and linebacker-type athletes have found themselves to be all-region Y-receivers after trying out for the position. Once this player is selected, he is asked to do many things for the offense. This player must be able to create mismatches for the defense. He needs to be able to use his size against smaller defensive backs and also be able to beat slow linebackers who try to cover him. He needs to be a very versatile player. He will be responsible for setting formation, lining up as a tight end, slot, and as a blocker in the backfield. He should have good hands and body control. He must be the best blocker on the team while also being able to get off of jams quickly at the line of scrimmage. He needs to be able to identify underneath coverage, which will help him find open areas on the field, and read secondary coverages and adjust vertical routes accordingly. This athlete is often most easily selected by looking first to the basketball team. Many power forwards have the intelligence, body control, and toughness to play the Y-receiver position, and these kinds of athletes usually quickly find the role to be exciting and thought-provoking.

H-Back

The H-back is given his position name because he is referred to as a hybrid. This athlete can often times be another Y-receiver, but he runs too fast and is more of a threat to run vertical route concepts. This player can be equally successful at blocking or route running and might even carry the football on runs plays a few times each game. This player is oftentimes one of the more well-rounded football players on a team. He is responsible to take on many tasks. He will need to be physical in getting off jams, block in the run game, be a legitimate weapon to run the ball, be a good route running with great hands, and be able to identify blitzes. This player must be good in traffic and willing to make the catch across the middle. He needs to be able to identify underneath coverage, which will help him find open areas on the field, and read secondary coverages and adjust vertical routes accordingly. This is a position where several different body types might be appropriate. In addition, if there is a question about who is best to play this position, sometimes the other players on the field can rotate into the H-back position without substituting new players into the game. This approach allows any athlete on the field to play there and utilize his skill sets. The H-back, then, is a very dynamic and versatile position.

T-Back

The T-back (or running back) is one of the best football players on the field. If this athlete can run and catch, then the team is made better. Some years, this position could be a big physical back or more of a pass catcher. The more versatile this athlete is, the better the team will be, but this player is at the T-back position because he is a great athlete. This player must be a threat both running and catching the ball. He must be able to move from the backfield into the slot and still be effective. The T-back must also be very football savvy as he is tasked with the responsibility of calling out protections and picking up the blitz.

Left Tackle

This player needs to be the best pass blocker on the team. He needs to have good feet and a long reach. He must have a quick first step and allow the quarterback time in the pocket.

In addition, because the air raid offense features so many screen plays, the left tackle needs to be able to get downfield and be agile enough to block smaller athletes in the screen game. When selecting an offensive line, the left tackle position should be reserved for the best athlete of that group. He will often be paired up with the defense's best rusher, and so he must be big enough, strong enough, and smart enough to handle that adversity.

Right Tackle

This player needs to have good size and be very strong. He should be both a good pass blocker and run blocker. He needs to be able to block down and have good enough feet to get downfield on chip blocks, or able to pick up smaller defensive backs in the screen game. This athlete is usually the second-best pass blocker and probably is not the left tackle because there is simply a better athlete who was available to place there.

Left Guard

The guards can generally be smaller and more agile than the tackles because they handle large athletes on the defense but not in space. These players do not have to move their feet with the same capabilities that the tackles must with rushers coming off the edge. It is preferable to find athletes who have strong upper bodies to slow the strong defensive tackle movements they will see on the interior of the line of scrimmage. In addition, these athletes will need to be able to pull in the run game, read defensive fronts, and understand the protection scheme.

Right Guard

The right guard is usually the less talented of the two guards. It is preferable to place the best lineman to the quarterback's blind side, and so the right guard does not need to be a great athlete. However, this player still needs to have good feet and be able to move quickly. He will need to be able to pull, read defensive fronts, and pick up the blitz. He also needs to be able to get downfield and pick up defenders in the screen game.

Center

The center is a position where the least physically talented lineman can be placed. This player can be small in size, but he must still be strong. He should have good hands and be athletic enough to make a shotgun snap while still picking up the correct block. He needs to have great footwork. However, while the center might be the smallest and least physically capable lineman, he probably has to be the most mentally astute of all five linemen. He is responsible for calling protection and reading the defensive front. He must be able to identify the blitz and make the correct protection call.

Conclusion

The air raid offense allows teams to compete no matter what the competition level. By having versatile athletes who can play in multiple formations and sets, the offense can dictate the style and pace of the game. Exploiting the weaknesses of a defense is one of the crucial keys to scoring points. Many defenses want to be able to substitute players so that they can tailor their defense to the down-and-distance situations. The ability to play with the 11 players on the field and avoid substitutions allows the offense to tailor its personnel to the situation while keeping the pace of the game fast and limiting the defense's ability to respond. The air raid offense allows the use of many different kinds of athletes. For example, the offense can use a wide variety of athletes at the Y-receiver. A 6'4", 220-pound athlete and a 5'7", 150-pound athlete both might play the Y-receiver position so that athletes can be shifted around the field to create favorable personnel match-ups all at a no-huddle pace. The ability to do this enables a fast-paced game of personnel groupings that the offense can dictate much to the detriment of defensive flexibility.

3

Practice Plan

A key to running a successful air raid offense is using practice time wisely. Getting as much practice in with tempo and hand signals will help teams prepare to play at a high level. In the air raid offense, the old adage *You play how you practice* rings true. It is imperative to instill the importance of getting lined up as soon as the referee spots the ball, hustling downfield during the play, not just waiting for the play to end, and finding the play caller on the sidelines after the play is over. The discipline of practicing this way during the week will pay off during games.

When constructing a weekly practice, all facets of the offense and all concepts for the day must be drilled in a very limited period of time. Each coach should know what specific skills and concepts need to be worked on each day. Therefore, the implementation of a useful practice plan for the week is a fundamental requirement in the air raid offense. It is not possible to get all the work in for a given week unless the time in practice is used wisely. The air raid offense is not a complex system, but it does require every skill set and each play type to be practiced a great deal in order to improve timing in game situations. Therefore, the practice schedule is broken up so that runs, screens, and passes are all run each day. A typical Monday practice may not include all the pass plays because there are too many to get done effectively in just one day (Figure 3-1). Generally, the strategy is to practice half of the quick passing game, dropback passing game, run game, and screen game on Monday, and then practice the other half of those play types on Tuesday. Therefore, different passes and runs are worked on during each day of the week. Tuesday's plan shows the second half of all those concepts being worked on in the same general time frames and in the same

Period	Time	QB	X/Z	H/Y	T	O-line
Pre-Practice	3:45–3:55	Soft toss	Pat-and-go	Pat-and-go	Circle handoffs	Centers: Snap G/T: Steps
Warm-Ups	3:55–4:05	Static stretch Dynamic stretch Calisthenics Warm-up arm	Static stretch Dynamic stretch Calisthenics	Static stretch Dynamic stretch Calisthenics	Static stretch Dynamic stretch Calisthenics	Static stretch Dynamic stretch Calisthenics
Individual	4:05–4:20	Three-step drops/reads Inside/outside zone handoffs and reads	Ball drills Jam release drills Quick routes	Ball drills Jam release drills Quick routes	Ball drills Ropes Inside/outside zone handoffs/reads	Stance and starts Zone steps
Screens	4:20–4:35	Ducks 1, 2, 3	Ducks 1, 2, 3	Ducks 1, 2, 3	Ducks 1, 2, 3	Ducks 1, 2, 3
Inside Runs/Mesh	4:35–4:50	Arizona Oakland	Arizona Oakland	Arizona Oakland	Arizona Oakland	Arizona Oakland
Routes on Air	4:50–5:20	Quick game: Houston, Hoosiers, Washington Dropbacks: Clemson, Texas Tech, Florida, Wyoming	Quick game: Houston, Hoosiers, Washington Dropbacks: Clemson, Texas Tech, Florida, Wyoming	Quick game: Houston, Hoosiers, Washington Dropbacks: Clemson, Texas Tech, Florida, Wyoming	Blitz pick-up	Quick game pass blocking
7-on-7	5:20–5:50	Quick game: Houston, Hoosiers, Washington Dropbacks: Clemson, Texas Tech, Florida, Wyoming	Quick game: Houston, Hoosiers, Washington Dropbacks: Clemson, Texas Tech, Florida, Wyoming	Quick game: Houston, Hoosiers, Washington Dropbacks: Clemson, Texas Tech, Florida, Wyoming	Quick game: Houston, Hoosiers, Washington Dropbacks: Clemson, Texas Tech, Florida, Wyoming	Zone run blocking
Team/Tempo	5:50–6:15	Quick game: Houston, Hoosiers, Washington Dropbacks: Clemson, Texas Tech, Florida, Wyoming Ducks 1, 2, 3 Runs: Arizona, Oakland	Quick game: Houston, Hoosiers, Washington Dropbacks: Clemson, Texas Tech, Florida, Wyoming Ducks 1, 2, 3 Runs: Arizona, Oakland	Quick game: Houston, Hoosiers, Washington Dropbacks: Clemson, Texas Tech, Florida, Wyoming Ducks 1, 2, 3 Runs: Arizona, Oakland	Quick game: Houston, Hoosiers, Washington Dropbacks: Clemson, Texas Tech, Florida, Wyoming Ducks 1, 2, 3 Runs: Arizona, Oakland	Quick game: Houston, Hoosiers, Washington Dropbacks: Clemson, Texas Tech, Florida, Wyoming

Figure 3-1. Monday practice plan

order (Figure 3-2). The Wednesday practice plan is structured to include all of the pass plays that need to be reviewed for the week along with any tags that might be utilized (Figure 3-3). The goal of the Wednesday practice is to get everything extra in for the week and to refine anything that was not done perfectly on Monday and Tuesday's practices. Thursday's practice plan will involve game-like situations of special teams and then a review of important pass plays, but all the plays will be run at the tempo that will be used on Friday night (Figure 3-4).

It is clearly visible that the practice plan incorporates a great deal of time for passing as the offense is a pass-first system. The balance achieved in each of these periods allows the offense to complete all of its skill sets each and every day. The key is to simply incorporate only portions of the offense each day so that each can have a fair amount of time dedicated to it. If a play is not going to be emphasized that week, then it can easily be moved out of the structure of the practice plan. This system is effective and allows the offense to move very quickly in practice so that the tempo that is to be achieved in games is practiced throughout the week. One final point is that the practice structure for Monday through Wednesday is basically kept exactly the same while only the plays run change. This is done intentionally in order to create in the minds of the athletes and the coaches a sense of familiarity and consistency. In the air raid offense, each member of the program should know the exact schedule for each practice and would only need to be told the individual pass or run concept that is due to be worked on during that day. This sense of structure enables the offense to move through practice more quickly and more efficiently because there is a common thread between each week's practices.

Pre-Practice

Pre-practice time is used to allow athletes to work on specific needs before the actual practice begins. During this period, all specialty players are practicing their skills. The field is divided into sections for punters, long snappers, return men, place kickers, and holders. If an athlete is not a specialty player, then he is working with his position coach on specific details that the coaching staff has identified for that week. For example, the quarterbacks can be using this time to warm up their arms and make the particular throws that the quarterback coach wants them to perfect for the week. This is a good opportunity to discuss game plans and new concepts/ideas and to work individually with the athletes.

Warm-Up

The warm-up phase of practice is critically important to the overall success of the practice structure. The offense operates at a very quick pace, and conditioning is an expectation during the drills that are performed throughout the daily practice routine. The period is maximized for productivity by separating the offense into their specific groups, thereby accelerating the warm-up process. Each coach should be responsible

Period	Time	QB	X/Z	H/Y	T	O-line
Pre-Practice	3:45–3:55	Soft toss	Pat-and-go	Pat-and-go	Circle handoffs	Centers: Snap G/T: Steps
Warm-Ups	3:55–4:05	Static stretch Dynamic stretch Calisthenics Warm-up arm	Static stretch Dynamic stretch Calisthenics	Static stretch Dynamic stretch Calisthenics	Static stretch Dynamic stretch Calisthenics	Static stretch Dynamic stretch Calisthenics
Individual	4:05–4:20	Three-step drops/ reads Five-step drops/reads Inside/outside zone handoffs and reads	Ball drills Jam release drills Vertical routes	Ball drills Jam release drills Vertical routes	Ball drills Ropes Power/counter handoffs and reads	Stance and starts Counter blocking Power blocking
Screens	4:20–4:35	Oregon 1, 2, 3	Oregon 1, 2, 3	Oregon 1, 2, 3	Oregon 1, 2, 3	Oregon 1, 2, 3
Inside Runs/Mesh	4:35–4:50	Pittsburgh Giants	Stock blocking Screen blocking	Pittsburgh Giants	Pittsburgh Giants	Pittsburgh Giants
Routes on Air	4:50–5:20	Quick game: Hawaii, Huskers, Hawkeye Dropbacks: Kansas, Georgia, Alabama	Quick game: Hawaii, Huskers, Hawkeye Dropbacks: Kansas, Georgia, Alabama	Quick game: Hawaii, Huskers, Hawkeye Dropbacks: Kansas, Georgia, Alabama	Blitz pick-up	Quick game pass blocking Screen blocking
7-on-7	5:20–5:50	Quick game: Hawaii, Huskers, Hawkeye Dropbacks: Kansas, Georgia, Alabama	Quick game: Hawaii, Huskers, Hawkeye Dropbacks: Kansas, Georgia, Alabama	Quick game: Hawaii, Huskers, Hawkeye Dropbacks: Kansas, Georgia, Alabama	Quick game: Hawaii, Huskers, Hawkeye Dropbacks: Kansas, Georgia, Alabama	Zone run blocking
Team/Tempo	5:50–6:15	Quick game: Hawaii, Huskers, Hawkeye Dropbacks: Kansas, Georgia, Alabama Ducks 1, 2, 3 Runs: Arizona, Oakland	Quick game: Hawaii, Huskers, Hawkeye Dropbacks: Kansas, Georgia, Alabama Ducks 1, 2, 3 Runs: Arizona, Oakland	Quick game: Hawaii, Huskers, Hawkeye Dropbacks: Kansas, Georgia, Alabama Ducks 1, 2, 3 Runs: Arizona, Oakland	Quick game: Hawaii, Huskers, Hawkeye Dropbacks: Kansas, Georgia, Alabama Ducks 1, 2, 3 Runs: Arizona, Oakland	Quick game: Hawaii, Huskers, Hawkeye Dropbacks: Kansas, Georgia, Alabama Ducks 1, 2, 3 Runs: Arizona, Oakland

Figure 3-2. Tuesday practice plan

Period	Time	QB	X/Z	H/Y	T	O-line
Pre-Practice	3:45–3:55	Soft toss	Pat-and-go	Pat-and-go	Circle handoffs	Centers: Snap G/T: Steps
Warm-Ups	3:55–4:05	Static stretch Dynamic stretch Calisthenics Warm-up arm	Static stretch Dynamic stretch Calisthenics	Static stretch Dynamic stretch Calisthenics	Static stretch Dynamic stretch Calisthenics	Static stretch Dynamic stretch Calisthenics
Individual	4:05–4:20	Three-step drops/ reads Five-step drops/reads Inside/outside zone handoffs and reads	Ball drills Jam release drills Vertical routes	Ball drills Jam release drills Vertical routes	Ball drills Ropes Power/counter handoffs and reads	Stance and starts Counter blocking Power blocking
Screens	4:20–4:35	Oregon 1, 2, 3 Ducks 1, 2, 3	Oregon 1, 2, 3 Ducks 1, 2, 3	Oregon 1, 2, 3 Ducks 1, 2, 3	Oregon 1, 2, 3 Ducks 1, 2, 3	Oregon 1, 2, 3 Ducks 1, 2, 3
Inside Runs/Mesh	4:35–4:50	Pittsburgh Giants Arizona Oakland	Stock blocking Screen blocking	Pittsburgh Giants Arizona Oakland	Pittsburgh Giants Arizona Oakland	Pittsburgh Giants Arizona Oakland
Routes on Air	4:50–5:20	Quick and vertical tags	Quick and vertical tags	Quick and vertical tags	Quick and vertical tags	Quick and vertical tags
7-on-7	5:20–5:50	Quick and vertical tags Ducks 1, 2, 3 Oregon 1, 2, 3	Quick and vertical tags Ducks 1, 2, 3 Oregon 1, 2, 3	Quick and vertical tags Ducks 1, 2, 3 Oregon 1, 2, 3	Quick and vertical tags Ducks 1, 2, 3 Oregon 1, 2, 3	Quick and vertical tags Ducks 1, 2, 3 Oregon 1, 2, 3
Team/Tempo	5:50–6:15	Quick and vertical tags Ducks 1, 2, 3 Oregon 1, 2, 3	Quick and vertical tags Ducks 1, 2, 3 Oregon 1, 2, 3	Quick and vertical tags Ducks 1, 2, 3 Oregon 1, 2, 3	Quick and vertical tags Ducks 1, 2, 3 Oregon 1, 2, 3	Quick and vertical tags Ducks 1, 2, 3 Oregon 1, 2, 3

Figure 3-3. Wednesday practice plan

Period	Time	QB	X/Z	H/Y	T	O-line
Pre-Practice	3:45–3:55	Soft toss	Pat-and-go	Pat-and-go	Circle handoffs	Centers: Snap G/T: Steps
Warm-Ups	3:55–4:05	Static stretch Dynamic stretch Calisthenics Warm-up arm	Static stretch Dynamic stretch Calisthenics	Static stretch Dynamic stretch Calisthenics	Static stretch Dynamic stretch Calisthenics	Static stretch Dynamic stretch Calisthenics
Kickoff/ Team Offense 80-Yard Drive	4:05–4:15	Ducks 1, 2, 3 Arizona Oakland	Ducks 1, 2, 3 Arizona Oakland	Ducks 1, 2, 3 Arizona Oakland	Ducks 1, 2, 3 Arizona Oakland	Ducks 1, 2, 3 Arizona Oakland
Kick Return/ Team Offense 80-Yard Tempo Drive	4:15–4:25	Quick game/tags Pittsburgh Giants	Quick game/tags Pittsburgh Giants	Quick game/tags Pittsburgh Giants	Quick game/tags Pittsburgh Giants	Quick game/tags Pittsburgh Giants
Punt/ Team Offense 80-Yard Tempo Drive	4:25–4:35	Vertical passing/tags	Vertical passing/tags	Vertical passing/tags	Vertical passing/tags	Vertical passing/tags
Punt Return/ Team Offense 80-Yard Tempo Drive	4:35–4:45	Call all plays	Call all plays	Call all plays	Call all plays	Call all plays
Extra Point Team Offense 20-Yard Drive	4:45–5:00	Red zone Goal line Two-point conversions	Red zone Goal line Two-point conversions	Red zone Goal line Two-point conversions	Red zone Goal line Two-point conversions	Red zone Goal line Two-point conversions

Figure 3-4. Thursday practice plan

for warming up his respective units. These groups include X- and Z-receivers, H- and Y-receivers, and quarterback and tailbacks. During the warm-up sessions, the groups take 15 minutes to run through calisthenics and stretching, both stationary and dynamic. While some individual groups may use the static stretch, the majority of the warm-up time is spent in a dynamic stretch to prepare the athletes' muscles for the movements that they will be expected to perform throughout the practice. Time is further maximized by having the entire group do the same exercise at the same time. After this session, coaches need to be sure their athletes are properly prepared for practice both mentally and physically.

Individual

Individual time is used to work in position groups to perfect each group's task for that given day. The coaches will follow the practice plan given for that day in terms of what skills to focus on in individual time. Each group should be working on the same core ideas, so when the units come together in team time, each position is up to speed. The introduction of a routine helps prepare both athletes and coaches for each session. As previously mentioned, the work is divided up into days on this practice structure. Therefore, each day, coaches work on a few specific aspects of the offense, with the goal of having everything worked on by Friday night. This allows for the offense to work effectively on all areas. For example, if all skill positions, linemen, and the quarterback are working on the quick game passes, they can use this individual time to perfect their route, reads, and blocking techniques related to those specific plays. Later in practice when the entire offensive unit comes together, the team will focus on those same routes as a unit. By using the individual time to practice the concept, the team can use team time to put it all together, while working on the no-huddle hand signals and tempo. This allows the offense to flow when the team time portion of the practice routine comes up each day.

Screens

Screens must be worked on every day, as they are an essential part of the air raid offense. The screen pass is used as a very effective way to move the ball. Screens typically take more practice because of the nature of the play. An offense with multiple screens will increase the chances of scoring, but also requires more practice time to perfect. These types of plays require choreography between all 11 players on the field at the exact same time. Therefore, screen sessions of practice need to be done as an entire unit because every position has a specific role to do. Working the entire unit together allows for the timing between the quarterback, receivers, and offensive linemen to improve each day. Using the entire unit also gives the blocking receiver experience with open field blocks, another crucial element to making the screen game effective. It is vital that all players are on the same page. A common strategy is to employ some of the second-team players or coaches to provide pressure on the quarterback to simulate real game experience. The offensive linemen are provided with targets downfield to aim at because downfield blocking may be a foreign concept to them. This session also allows the receivers to practice catching the ball on screens. Many times, the receiver will have to catch the ball in traffic, or with his back downfield, which may cause some problems for him. By working on the screen game every day, an offense can work multiple screens and tags off of those screens. Using screens to set up big downfield plays can get an offense some easy yards and scores. It is essential to set the defense to react quickly to try to stop the screen for short yardage. By doing so, the offense can now run play-action off the screen and get a receiver behind the fast-reacting defense. The only way to get these extra yards and scores is by being effective in the screen game and forcing the defense to react to the screen. That simulated game situation must be practiced every day in order for the offense to become productive.

Inside Run

The inside run session of practice gives the offensive line, quarterback, tailback, and slots (H/Y) a chance to work on running the ball against an opponent's defense. During this session, a scout defense needs to present the offense with the different fronts and stunts they may possibly see during game day. This session is done every day, while focusing on a few runs each day, with the idea of working on all runs by the end of the week. The easiest way to accomplish this is to focus alternating days on the zone running plays and gap scheme running plays. This allows the offensive linemen to work on the two main run blocking systems that will be utilized in the air raid offense, but be able to maximize repetitions each day on a limited number of concepts. Inside run periods are often done at a slower pace that some of the other periods during the practice. The defense will inevitably try to confuse the offense by stemming and lining up in multiple fronts. Taking time to ensure all positions know their responsibility every play will lead to greater degrees of success for the offense. This session is also important for the H-back position to practice the down blocking, fold blocking, and the possibility of running the ball as an effective weapon for the offense. During this time, the quarterback needs to be practicing identifying the defensive blitzes and communicating to his coaching staff what he is seeing. He needs to act as a coach on the field. The inside run section of practice is pivotal to creating and effective run game to complement the air raid's passing attack.

Routes on Air

The routes on air session is the time built into the practice plan for route perfection. The offensive skill unit should work on the pass plays that are to be emphasized that day from every formation the offense wants to be proficient with for that week. The air raid pass routes are concept-based, meaning that each receiver's route is extremely important regardless of whether the pass is thrown to them or not. Giving the receivers and quarterback time to work on their timing, spacing, and communication will increase productivity on the field. The receivers and quarterback must be on the same page for each route; if the receivers' spacing is wrong, two receivers may be covered by one defender, making that route ineffective. This session is also a good opportunity for the quarterback and receivers to practice reading coverages. Many of the air raid pass plays require both the receiver and quarterback to read whether or not the defense is playing cover 2 or cover 3. The receivers' route will change, depending on the defensive coverage; if the quarterback reads a specific coverage and the receiver reads a different coverage, the possible result is a turnover. This period is a teaching period, so pace is sometimes sacrificed, but the period will move as quickly as it is possible to move without sacrificing accuracy.

During the routes on air session, a scout defense will be showing different coverages to give the quarterback and receivers the opportunity to read those coverages and their nuances. The defense is encouraged to show a certain coverage and then switch late to another coverage to give the effect of a defense stemming pre-snap. This session should be focused more on coaching and corrections as opposed to tempo, but as previously stated, speed is still important when possible. During this time, the offensive coaches should move multiple players to different positions to become a more dangerous offense and encourage cross training of the athletes. This cross-training is done to help develop multiple athletes who can play multiple positions, thereby making the offense more versatile and less susceptible to injuries. In addition, this helps keep the best athletes on the field. When receivers play other positions, it also allows them to understand the concept of the route and the importance of each route in the greater concept of the offense.

7-on-7

The air raid offense practice routine features a 7-on-7 period every day. This session is an opportunity for the offensive skill players to run their routes against a live defensive shell. The route concepts called during 7-on-7 should be the same route concepts that were previously reviewed during the routes on air period. The two periods are built into the practice plan back-to-back to ensure that the skilled players are immersed in as much time actually running routes and catching footballs as possible. The offense should simulate the tempo used on game night during this period. This tempo allows the quarterback and receivers to practice getting the formation and play from the sidelines by hand signals and then executing the play. There is absolutely no need to stop plays for coaching during this period. This should be a live speed full-tempo drill, and any coaching points should be documented and retained for a later time so that tempo is not disrupted. If an athlete needs to be corrected, or is fatigued, he should be substituted out quickly and returned to the drill after there is a stoppage of play because of a score. The 7-on-7 period should emulate game-like situations as much as possible with the only breaks coming when there is a turnover or a score. The ball should be spotted at different positions on the field, including both hash marks and the middle of the field and on random yard lines. This will give the receivers experience of finding the line of scrimmage and making sure they are aligned properly for the next play. It is good practice to put a manger or coach in charge of spotting the ball and make sure he has two or three extra footballs so that each time there is an incompletion or the ball is lost, a new one can be spotted immediately and the tempo maintained.

Team Tempo

The team tempo period is a session for the entire offensive unit. The rationale behind this period is to simulate a game experience in every way practically possible. All coaches should be off the field, and the ball should be spotted as if it were a game. This gives the entire offensive unit practice at reading hand signals, lining up in proper alignment, and moving as fast as possible to the ball. Each play worked on that day or week should be called at some point during the team time. Some coaches might find it helpful to use a script during this period if that is applicable to how the game would actually be called in a real-life situation. This gives the athletes the opportunity to perfect the plays that will be called on game night. The tempo should remain at game speed, so substitutions should only take place in case of an injury or else restricted until after a change of possession or a score. If substituting should be done at some point, it should happen from the sidelines, and then only in cases when it would be performed during a game. The team tempo period is when a no-huddle air raid offense must fine-tune the skills needed to be a real tempo team. These are great sessions to film and utilize during film session with the team at another time. It is critical that everything is done exactly how a team wants their game situations to look.

Conclusion

The old adage of practicing the way you play is fundamentally important when implementing the air raid offense. This system is very sensitive to minor changes and must be constantly reviewed and practiced in order to account for variable on game night. It is essential that the skills that athletes are asked to perform on game nights are performed exactly the same way throughout the week during practice. This conformity breeds confidence among the players and encourages them to feel confident when going into a contest. In short, practicing effectively during the week will translate into big points on game night. Using the practice time given to implement everything for the week can be a daunting task; breaking down the practice into sessions will help to ensure that everything gets covered. A well-constructed practice plan that informs athletes and coaches exactly what tasks or skills they are to perform in a set time frame will make sure that everyone on the program is time on task and performing at an optimum level. The structure of the practice plan should not be altered. It is essential that the athletes and coaches fall into a routine so that they know what is expected of them each day. The plays inside the session can and do easily change to fit the needs of specific opponents in a given week but the overall stability in the structure of the practice plan lends itself to a well-coordinated program necessary for offensive success.

4

Formations

A well-constructed air raid offense requires the ability to run multiple formations sets and motions at a defense. The ability to execute multiple sets, while still maintaining a high tempo, will force defenses into basic coverages. Oftentimes, this results in defenses not having the time to make the proper adjustments or substitutions. Each formation used is designed to serve a specific purpose in the overall scheme of the offense. Some of these formations are used to help the concept of the route work more effectively, while others are designed to try to force a mismatch against the defense.

This chapter was designed to show the reader the basic structure of the formations most often utilized in the air raid offense. The hand signals that quickly move the players into these formations will be discussed in Chapter 7. Several things are done structurally to enable the athletes to move into position more effectively and more quickly. First, the X- and Z-receivers very seldom change sides of the field. The X-receiver almost exclusively plays on the left side of the formation, while the Z-receiver plays on the right side of the formation. These two athletes have the longest distance to run, so it is essential that they are not forced to change sides of the field often in order to facilitate their quick progress to the line of scrimmage. These two athletes will simply identify the Y-receiver. If the Y-receiver is to their side of the formation, then they know to back off the line of scrimmage and play as a flanker. If the Y-receiver is on the opposite side of the formation, then they are aware that they will have to step up onto the line of scrimmage and play as the split end receiver.

This system greatly reduces the amount of information that they have to know and how often they have to move around the field. The Y-receiver knows where to line up based upon the hand signal, but also by the hand used by the signal caller. If the signal caller uses his right hand, which is signified with a red armband, then the Y-receiver knows he will be setting the formation to the right. If the signal caller uses the left hand, signified by a yellow armband, then the Y-receiver will set the formation to the left. The H-back always sets his position relative to the Y-receiver. On all 2x2 formations, the H-back knows he will line up on the opposite side of the ball from the Y-receiver. If the formation is a 3x1 set, then the H-back lines up on the same side as the Y-receiver and identifies the hand signal to tell him exactly where. There are no hand signals for the T-back except an empty hand signal. He must know where to line on each play based upon the formation called. This system has allowed air raid teams to get lined up quickly in a variety of sets and move to the line with purpose to confuse and attack defenses more effectively.

These formations are all shown to the right for the purpose of simplicity. These would all be right hand signals or red armband signals. These formations could all be flipped and run to the left side by using the same hand signal with the left hand, signified by a yellow armband on the left arm.

2x2 Formations

The base formation in the air raid offense is a 2x2 formation with the X- and Z-receivers playing on or near the top of the numbers on the high school field and the H-back splitting the difference between the X-receiver and the offensive tackle. The Y-receiver will flex his alignment to any width he feels is necessary for him to execute his assignment (Figure 4-1).

The Y-receiver can also line up as a true tight end and provide the offense with some advantages in the run game as well as altering how he can be covered in the passing attack. This formation would be called 2x2 tight right (Figure 4-2). No one else is affected except the Y-receiver in this formational grouping.

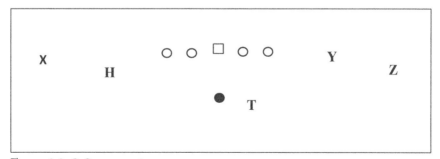

Figure 4-1. 2x2 open set

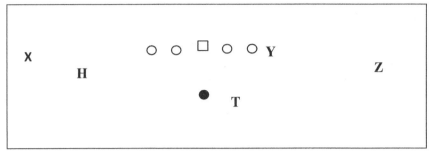

Figure 4-2. 2x2 tight set

A benefit may be had from time to time in having the H-back line up as a wingback away from the Y-receiver. This is accomplished by the H-back cutting down his alignment to a wing, two yards off the tackle, and one yard into the backfield on the opposite side of the ball from the Y-receiver (Figure 4-3). It is also very easy to keep the H-back in that wingback alignment and move the Y-receiver into a true tight end position with another simple change of hand signal (Figure 4-4). This formation is a combination of the previous two formations. This formation structure still allows all passes to be run while also helping improve blocking angles in the run game. This formation can also help some of the timing on mesh routes and also make the H-back a potential threat to run the ball.

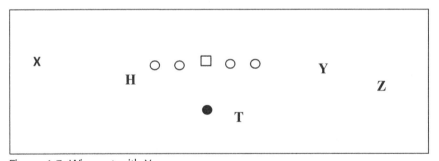

Figure 4-3. Wing set with Y open

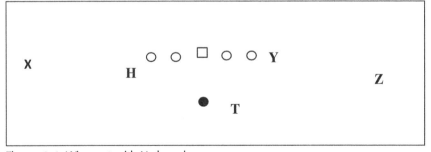

Figure 4-4. Wing set with Y closed

In several instances, teams might choose to utilize man coverage against the air raid offense. When this happens, it is necessary to compress the formations in order to create natural rubs on the defenders. The 2x2 formation that allows this to be done most effectively is called 2x2 stack (Figure 4-5). In this formation, the receivers stack behind one another. The H- and Y-receivers set the formation by both being on the line. The X- and Z-receivers line up directly behind them. This structure allows the offense to run all its plays while causing assignment conflicts for the defense. Many teams will refuse to stay in a man coverage look against this formation, and it also enables the X- and Z-receivers to have clean release from the line of scrimmage without being jammed by a defender. This formation is also good when running double move routes and crossing routes because of the release angles that the receivers have next to one another.

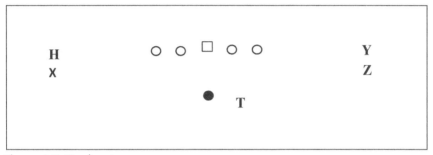

Figure 4-5. Stack set

Recently, it has become popular to use more unconventional sets in the air raid offense. Defenses are quickly becoming accustomed to the 2x2 and 3x1 structures of the offense, and so variations of these structures often causes alignment issues for the defense and give the offense a numerical superiority. One such formation that creates these mismatches is the nasty formation (Figure 4-6). In this formation, the Y-receiver will line up in a three-point stance, with an extra wide split from the tackle, and the H-back will fill that open space one yard off the ball. This formation provides the offense with a great advantage to run the ball outside. In addition, most of the pass plays can still be very effective from this set. Any delay routes or slow screens will benefit from the use of this formation.

The final 2x2 formation used in the air raid offense is the 2x2 empty set (Figure 4-7). This formation is the same as the base 2x2 formation, but moves the T-back to a receiver, lined up between the slot and the tackle. This formation will present a possible mismatch between a fast T-back and a slower linebacker. This formation is also effective when motioned from a base 2x2 structure into an empty set.

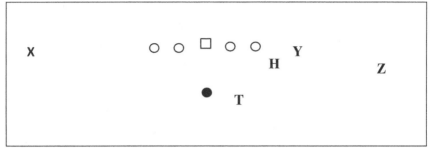

Figure 4-6. Nasty set

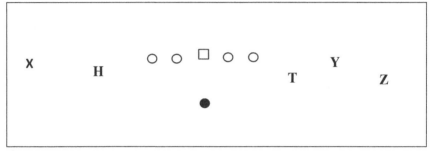

Figure 4-7. Empty set

3x1 Formations

The 3x1 structure is used to outnumber defenses to the wide side of the field, create a three-receiver route concept, or to isolate a great receiver to the short side of the field. The first formation is the base 3x1 formation (Figure 4-8). This formation is typically called to the wide side of the field. The Y-receiver sets the formation by being on the line of scrimmage and near the hash mark. He will alter his split based upon the concept called by a few yards. The outside receiver (either X or Z, depending on the call) should be on the inside of the numbers, while the H-back splits the difference between the Y-receiver and the offensive tackle. This formation is good for flooding the wide side of the field, running quick screens, and also pushing vertical.

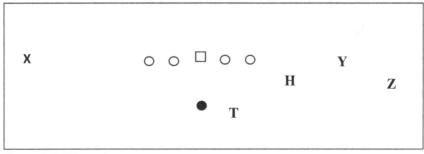

Figure 4-8. Trips set

From time to time, an advantage can result in placing the Y-receiver as the inside receiver and allowing the H-back to play the #2 receiver position. This structure is accomplished by calling a 3x1 invert formation (Figure 4-9). This formation will allow for the same route concepts to be run. The inverted structure will also give the more athletic H-back greater access to more routes so that he can cause the defense more coverage issues.

Distinct advantages can also result in keeping the Y-receiver in a tight end position while also maintaining a 3x1 alignment. This 3x1 tight formation is very versatile in that it allows the offense to have an extra blocker in the run game while also having three receivers on the line of scrimmage to one side of the formation (Figure 4-10).

Defenses often attempt to alter their alignment based upon match-ups. They will get close to receivers that they feel they can cover deep and play off receivers that they are worried might beat them on deep route concepts. In order to take advantage of this strategy, the air raid offense will employ the 3x1 bunch formation (Figure 4-11).

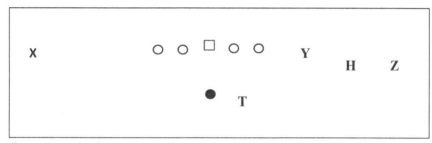

Figure 4-9. Trips invert set

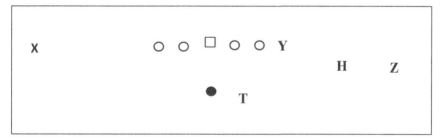

Figure 4-10. Trips with Y closed

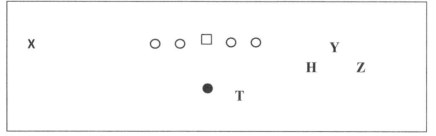

Figure 4-11. Bunch set

This formation can be set near the offensive tackle or out on the hash mark based upon what the offense is attempting to do to the defense. This helps with blocking the outside zone run, shortens the throw for the quick screens, and allows the offense to run quick screens into the boundary. In addition, some route concepts are actually better run from this compressed alignment because of the nature of how they attack defensive coverage structures. If the formation is called to the boundary, then the backside receiver will have the entire field side to beat his man in coverage.

The bunch formation has been a great asset to air raid teams for many years. There are times where the offense can gain an advantage from staying in a 3x1 alignment but only bunching two of the receivers. This formation is called a broken bunch formation (Figure 4-12). This structure keeps the slot receivers—with the Y-receiver being on the line of scrimmage—in the bunch formation, while moving the Z-receiver back out to his original split. This is another way to get the same route combinations with different starting points. This formation can also be achieved by starting in the bunch set and motioning the Z-receiver out to his position. The formation often causes defenses to stretch or stress their coverage in order to adequately cover both the Z-receiver in space and the compressed alignment of the Y-receiver and H-back. This is a great formation in that it provides the best of both worlds of a spread and compressed formation structure.

The final 3x1 formation is an empty set with three receivers to the callside and a single receiver and the T-back to the weakside (Figure 4-13). This formation provides an empty set with three receivers all sharing one side of the formation. Oftentimes, this structure will cause the defense to distort or even change altogether their base coverage assignments. In addition, this formation will allow the tailback into his pass route more quickly.

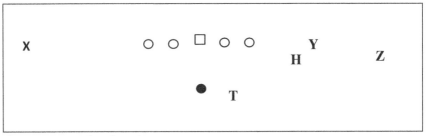

Figure 4-12. Broken bunch set

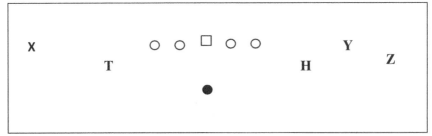

Figure 4-13. 3x1 empty set

Special Formations

The air raid offense operates principally from fairly standard 2x2 and 3x1 formations the majority of the time. However, there are times where special formations are needed either in situational football, to give the defense an alternate look at a play that is run often, or to help in an area that the offense may be struggling in during a game. One such formation is a standard I formation set that allows the quarterback to go under center and utilize a two-back backfield to increase the potency of the running game (Figure 4-14). It is possible to substitute a fullback into the game, but it is better to utilize the H-back or Y-receiver in the lead blocker role in order to maintain a quick tempo. The Y-receiver can also play as a tight end or as a slotback based upon what is needed. This formation allows the offense to change structure and style very quickly while maintaining tempo. It is very difficult for defenses to match the change of style with the personnel group they have on the field to defend the shotgun sets that the offense normally operates. This allows the offense to utilize the formation and quickly switch back to spread sets and keep the defense off balance.

The split formation provides a way to run the two-back system with a shotgun set (Figure 4-15). The H-back moves from the slot to the backfield on the opposite side of the quarterback from the T-back. All plays can still be called in this formation. The spilt formation will help with the run game by providing a lead blocker, or having an option threat. This formation gives a balanced look, which will not give the defense a key on the run game.

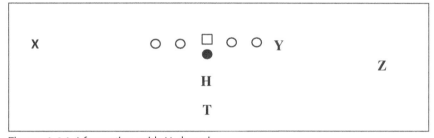

Figure 4-14. I formation with Y closed

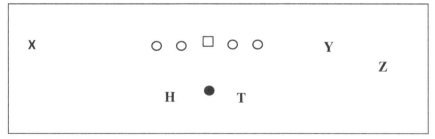

Figure 4-15. Split set

The quattro (or 4x1) formation allows the offense to create a wide array of structural mismatches for defenses (Figure 4-16). The receivers will line up in their base 3x1 formation, and the T will then line up between the H and the offensive tackle, which gives the offense four receivers to the callside. This will cause the defense to make coverage adjustments, while getting single coverage on the X-receiver. This formation is great in calling mesh routes to the field, quick screen to the field, 1-on-1 routes to the boundary, and allows the T-back to block down in order to facilitate rollout passes by the quarterback.

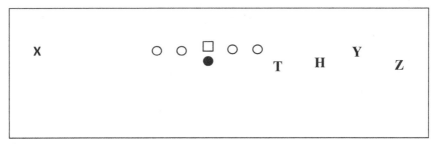

Figure 4-16. Quattro set

The great white formation is a two-tight-end structure (Figure 4-17). This structure allows the offense to run a power run attack out of the shotgun. Any pass play can still be called, along with multiple play-action passes. The Y-receiver and H-back will line up in tight end positions, while the X- and Z-receivers will both serve as flankers. The X- and Z-receivers can also be placed to the same side of the formation while maintaining the two-tight-end structures in an ace over formation (Figure 4-18). This

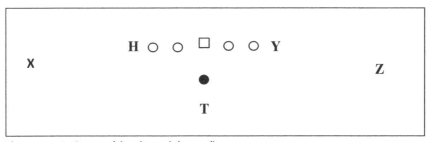

Figure 4-17. Great white (two-tight-end) set

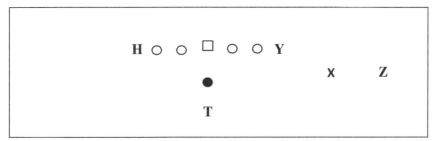

Figure 4-18. Great white over set

allows for the offense's two fastest athletes to run combination routes while maintaining the advantage of the extra blockers up front.

The final special formation used in the air raid offense is the buccaneer formation (Figure 4-19). This structure is relatively new to the air raid offense in that it uses the pistol alignment of the T-back. The T-back is the principal running back, and the H-back moves into the backfield as a leader blocker.

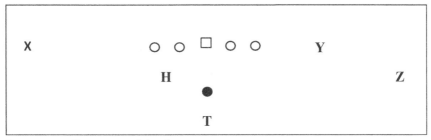

Figure 4-19. Buccaneer (pistol) set

Conclusion

The use of multiple formations in the air raid offense allows for maximum offensive production. The variable formation structure of the offense requires that there be adequate practice time set aside to install each route combination with each formation. While this does require some extensive training during the installation of the offense, the athletes quickly grasp the simplicity and commonality of the formations, and less time is devoted to practicing formations as a season progresses. The use of multiple formations keeps the offense from becoming predictable and forces defenses to devote large amounts of time to recognition of formations instead of strategies for stopping plays.

5

No-Huddle Communication— Formations

The no-huddle allows an offense to move at an increased pace and destroy the ability of defense to substitute personnel. There are two main reasons to prevent defensive substitutions. First, it prevents the defense from getting injured or fatigued athletes off the field. If the opposition tries to send on new players, they will be caught with too many players on the field when the ball is snapped. The quarterback must be trained to snap the ball and run the play if he sees defensive players attempting a substitution into the game. The second reason to play at an increased pace is to prevent the defense from changing the configuration, structure, and personnel of their defense. The 11 athletes the offense has on the field can get into multiple formation sets. This allows the offense to change formation and structure rapidly, without substituting, while the defense may be caught with too few or too many of a certain type of player on the field. For example, the offense can utilize a wide variety of spread sets, but has cross-trained the Y-receiver to play the fullback position on the field. This will allow the offense to change from a spread set to a two-back power set on the fly and prevent the defense from substituting bigger defensive personnel into the game to stop the run.

The no-huddle is a major component of what makes the air raid offense such a viable threat to defenses. This is a major reason why the offense limits how many plays to run and attempts to keep the formations and substitutions to a manageable number. It is important to note that the no-huddle is a communication tool that must be practiced at every opportunity. A good no-huddle team will play in this communication structure during 7-on-7, team time, drill periods almost exclusively.

Communicating Formations

When employing an air raid offense at no-huddle tempo, the first thing that must be considered is how to signal the information to the athletes. One of the easiest and most effective ways to signal this information into the game is with a series of hand signals. The first major piece of information that has to be conveyed to the athletes on the field is the formation. The average air raid team may wish to employ a wide variety of formations, and so it is essential that these formations are conveyed in a very expedient manner. The coach who does the signaling wears a red armband on his right wrist and a yellow armband on his left wrist so that the athletes on the field can see the color and immediately know if the formation is meant to be set to the right or to the left. Multiple signalers are used in a game to relay the information, but all wear the same red and yellow armbands and all signal the same formation simultaneously to ensure that the athletes quickly line up in that set to expedite the transition from one play to the next. A common theme is then established between each formation to make them more recognizable from the sideline and easier to remember. A concerted effort is made to make the hand signal relate in the athletes' minds so that they remember the common themes throughout all the formations.

The air raid offense uses a variety of 2x2 or balanced formations and so all 2x2 formations will utilize the two-finger or "devil horn" hand signal (Figure 5-1). All formations that utilize a 2x2 set are then going to be a variation of that one hand signal. Anytime a coach holds up those two fingers, it will automatically mean the team is in a 2x2 set with the Y-receiver and H-back lined up on opposite sides of the ball. This one hand signal then conveys a great deal of information, and the derivatives of it can help create many formations. If the devil horn is held up with the right hand, which

Figure 5-1. 2x2 hand signal

is signified with a red armband, then the Y-receiver will set the formation to the right, and the H-back will go to the left. If the left hand was held up, signified with a yellow armband, then the Y-receiver would move the formation to the left while the H-back went to the right. The X- and Z-receivers never have to change sides and just move up or back off the line of scrimmage relative to the position of the Y-receiver. This approach helps to speed up how quickly the athletes can get themselves lined up into a particular formation.

If the devil horn is then pulled tight to the chest with the right hand, the result will be the Y-receiver being in a tight end position (Figure 5-2). Anytime the formation is pulled tight to the chest, it sends a common theme that the Y-receiver is meant to be in a tight end alignment. These common themes inside the formations help the athletes to remember the formations and tags off of them more quickly. If the devil horn signal wrist (right hand) is held by the opposite hand, then the Y-receiver will be to the right and the H-back will be set as a wingback away from the Y-receiver (Figure 5-3). The left hand holding the right wrist helps to make the arms look like a "chicken wing" and so thereby helps to make the H-back think of being in a wing alignment. Anytime the wrist is grabbed by the offhand, then the H-back is being told to line up as a wingback. If the right wrist is held while making the devil horn and then pulled tight to the chest, the result will be the Y-receiver moving to a tight alignment while the H-back is a wingback away (Figure 5-4). If the devil horn is made with both hands and used in a stacking motion one on top of the other, then the result is a stack set with one receiver lined up directly behind the other receiver (Figure 5-5). If the formation desired is a nasty set in a 2x2 structure, the coach will hold his nose with the hand that he wants the Y-receiver to move toward (Figure 5-6). The final 2x2 set used is a 2x2 empty package. The athletes will be provided with a devil horn in the direction desired to go. The empty aspect of the formation will be relayed by the signaling coach rubbing his stomach (the sign for empty) and then pointing which direction the T-back is desired to line up (Figure 5-7).

Figure 5-2. 2x2 with a closed tight end set

Figure 5-3. 2x2 with a wingback set

Figure 5-4. 2x2 with the tight end closed and a wingback set

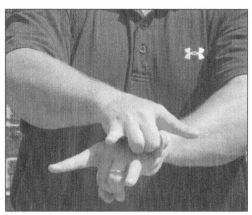

Figure 5-5. Stack set

Figure 5-6. Nasty set

Figure 5-7. Empty set

The 3x1 (or trips) formations are handled in the same style as 2x2 sets. Three fingers will be held aloft on whichever hand the trips formation is to be set to. If the trips formation is to be set to the right, then three fingers are held up on the right hand signified by the red armband (Figure 5-8). The 3x1 formation set can then be adjusted as follows:
- Bring in tight with the hand to the chest (Figure 5-9).
- Invert with the fingers held down (Figure 5-10).
- Compress into a bunch set with the three fingers squeezed by the opposite hand (Figure 5-11).
- Place into a loose or broken bunch by flashing the three fingers and then acting as if they are being broken (Figure 5-12).
- Place into an empty set by flashing three fingers to one side and then rubbing the stomach and pointing opposite the formation for the T-back (Figure 5-13).

Figure 5-8. Trips set

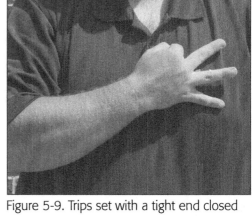
Figure 5-9. Trips set with a tight end closed

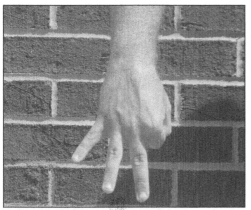
Figure 5-10. Inverted trips set

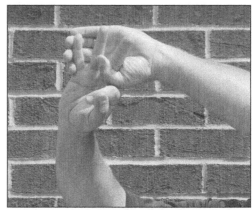
Figure 5-11. Bunch set

Figure 5-12. Broken bunch set

Figure 5-13. Trips empty set

The offense also employs a wide variety of other formations that just utilize a separate hand signal. For instance, if the desire is to line up in a two-back I formation set, then the coach will just point to his eye with the hand direction that he wants the Y-receiver to go to (Figure 5-14). A split back set is created with a vertical hand splitting the signaling coach's body (Figure 5-15). An advantage may be gained from time to time by the offense moving into a two-back pistol set. This is achieved by covering one eye with the hand in order to signify an eye patch, as this call set is known as buccaneer (Figure 5-16). A 4x1 (or quattro) set is signaled by putting up a fist to obviate the international signal of fourth down (Figure 5-17). Recently, great deals of two-tight-end sets have been utilized known as the great white formation. The signal for great white is simply a fin above the head (Figure 5-18). If this two-tight-end set calls for the flankers to both align to the same side, then the great white sign is given and then the signaler points to the side he wants both flankers to move to (Figure 5-19).

Figure 5-14. I formation set

Figure 5-15. Split set

Figure 5-16. Buccaneer set

Figure 5-17. Quattro set

Figure 5-18. Great white set

Figure 5-19. Great white over set

Motion Signals

The air raid offense features a no-huddle tempo and attempts to force the defense into bad situations with the speed of its attack. There is a need, from time to time, to utilize motion in order to distort the defense's understanding of the offensive structure. Motion should be a weapon that is used with a purpose. If the scouting report of a particular team shows that no advantage is gained by the use of the motion, then it is better to play fast and not waste time motioning. However, if a distinct advantage is to be gained, then the offense should utilize it, even if it reduces the speed at which a play is able to run.

Motion hand signals must be made very simple for the athletes to recognize and remember. The hand signal that is most symbolic of motion is that of a hand playing the piano (Figure 5-20). If this movement is made with one hand, then the called receiver will motion in toward the ball but stay on his side of the field. If the same movement is made with both hands, then player will motion all the way across the

Figure 5-20. Motion hand signal

formation and pass the football. Each skilled position player on the field must be given a hand signal designation that means he is being spoken to by the signal caller. These signals can vary from game to game, as long as each skilled player knows which signal is speaking to him. The motion hand signal stays consistent so that whenever an athlete sees his tag signal and then the piano hands, then he knows to go in motion. Several other motion signals can be used, but they are all based upon and start with the piano hands signal.

Conclusion

All of these formations can be seen in Chapter 6. These are a sample of some of the most commonly used formations in the air raid offense. These formations are certainly not a comprehensive list of the formations that a coach might wish to employ, but they give a cross section of some of the more useful formations that are generally used each year. An almost limitless number of formations can be used because of the simplicity of signaling and common themes built within the signaling structure. There are many ways to signal in the formations, but the key component is that the system be simple and one that the athletes can understand very quickly.

6

No-Huddle Communication— Plays

The air raid offense operates at its most effective level when it is in what is called *tempo*. Tempo comes in several forms. The slowest is known as the look tempo (or check-with-me) tempo, where the play is hand-signaled in, and the entire team sees the hand signal and then gets in a stance and plays. The second tempo is called fastball tempo, which is a no-huddle concept in which the play is signaled in using hand signals from the sideline for the skill players and is communicated verbally to the offensive linemen by the quarterback. A third form of tempo is referred to as racehorse tempo, where a code word is just yelled out to the players and they run that predetermined play that corresponds to the call. There are many ways to change this tempo and slow the game down or speed it up. The basis of this chapter is to explain the fastball tempo. The fastball tempo is the primary way in which many no-huddle teams today operate today. There are many ways to signal this, but the following illustrations and codes are what have worked well in the past.

Rationale of Signaling Plays

When plays are signaled in to an offense, they have to be renamed. Defenses and their coaches are very smart and always on the lookout to try to devise what an offense is attempting to do to them. For that reason, the offense must rename all the plays that will be called into the game. If the offense called its hitch/corner play a "smash," then the defense would quickly learn what that means as most spread offense run some version of a smash concept. Therefore, smash must be given a new identity so that

when it is signaled in and verbalized by the quarterback, it is encoded. In order for athletes to understand the hand signals and what is being asked of them, it is necessary to create a common learning theme behind each play, for example:
- Runs: Pro sports cities/mascots
- Screens: University of Oregon Ducks
- Quick/dropback Passes: College football teams/mascots

These categories allow the offense to be stripped down to its most basic concepts and communicated in an effective manner. When the plays are coded in this manner, then no one on the defense will understand what is being communicated. If a play name is changed from say "flood" to being called and signaled as "Texas," then that word will tell the offense all that they need to know, but will leave the defense guessing as to what the call means. In addition, these signals allow the play to be audibled effectively by the quarterback at the line of scrimmage. When the quarterback says the code word "Texas," it only relates information to the offense and is encoded to the defense.

Run Play Signals

The key to making the hand signals work is to create a signal that very closely associates the call with the play. For example, if the play is jet sweep, which is a run play, then the signal category is a pro sports city. The common bond on this is pretty simple, as the play has the word "Jet" inside of it, and the New York Jets are an NFL team. Therefore, the hand signal for this play, if it is to be run to the right, is to make a motion of a jet taking flight with the right hand (Figure 6-1). This hand signal creates a very simple connection in the athletes' minds, as they know the play is called "jet sweep" and there is a pro sports city that hosts the Jets. The quarterback will verbalize at the line of scrimmage the word *jet* and another code word that gives the direction, or he may use a predetermined derivative of the call, such as "New York" as the Jets play in that city. This conveys all the information to the offense that they require, but keeps the play concept and direction hidden from the defense.

Figure 6-1. Jet sweep hand signal

Screen Play Signals

Screens are an integral part of the air raid offense and actually take up more plays than the run game most years. In order to keep the number of hand signals simple, the screens are all placed into one common theme, for example, the University of Oregon Ducks. Three quick screen concepts are utilized by many air raid teams, and so these three screens are just labeled as Ducks 1, 2, and 3. Ducks 1 means the ball will be thrown to the #3 receiver on a bubble screen, Ducks 2 means the screen will go to the outside receiver based upon formation, and the Ducks 3 call means the ball is thrown to the tailback. Ducks 1 is simply a bubble screen to the inside receiver in the formation with the #1 receiver blocking the outside defender and the #2 receiver blocking for the #3 receiver. This is a pretty standard play among all spread offenses. The hand signal is very simple: the signaler will make a duck feathers signal with the hand that corresponds to the side he wants the screen thrown to and then simply hold up the number of the screen to be run (Figure 6-2). This significantly cuts down on the number of play signals that have to be remembered. All Ducks hand signals are quick screens, and so all the players have to know is which number of the Ducks family is called. A set of hand signals will then tell the offense which side to run the play to. These hand signals can be whatever a coach feels signifies left or right in the athletes' minds.

Figure 6-2. Ducks screen hand signal

Pass Play Signals

The air raid offense is a pass-first system, and so a great deal of time is spent signaling pass plays to the offensive personnel. For that reason, the pass plays are categorized as college teams and/or mascots. This is done for the simple reason that there are more collegiate teams and mascots to choose from than pro sports cities. The goal was for there to be an almost limitless number of pass play hand signals to be utilized. One of the base air raid plays over the years has been the mesh concept. This pass play was made famous by coach Hal Mumme during his tenure at the University of Kentucky. Therefore, the hand signal becomes a version of Kentucky. When the mesh play is called, it is renamed Kentucky. The hand signal requires the signaling coach to make two Ks with his hands turned sideways across his chest (Figure 6-3). This signal means that the entire offense knows the Kentucky concept is being called, but the defense has no idea what Kentucky means or what play to be run is based upon the signal. The quarterback can verbalize the word "Kentucky" or some version of it that has been pre-approved during practice that week.

Figure 6-3. Kentucky pass play hand signal

Quarterback Communication at the Line of Scrimmage

The hand signals are a great way for the five skill players and the quarterback to see the play call. However, the offensive linemen need to be in their stance while the signaling is going on to facilitate the ball being snapped at a quicker tempo. This means that the quarterback is responsible for telling the offensive linemen what the play is and what direction it will be going. This is accomplished by incorporating the same common theme system that was used to originally create the hand signals. If the play that is signaled in is Jets, then the quarterback will audible a code word that means Jets to the offensive linemen. Several different words must be learned over the course of the season for plays that will be called repeatedly in games. A great example would be the term New York, which is where the Jets play football. If the quarterback comes to the line of scrimmage and calls the term "New York," then the linemen will know that it is the Jets play being called from the sideline. This can be done in a myriad of ways, of course. Another word might be "Brooklyn," "Empire," or "Apple" because all of these words have to do with the city of New York and bring the athletes back to the theme of Jets. The number of these words that can be used is limited only by the ability of players to accurately remember them. Pass plays are not required to be so well-disguised, but run plays need several different words to activate them.

The final thing the quarterback must do is to give a play direction to the offensive linemen. This is done with the colored armbands in the hand signal for the skilled players but again the linemen do not see those signals. If the play is supposed to be jet sweep to the right, then the quarterback would call "Apple south." Apple would tell the linemen it is jet sweep, and "south" and/or "west" would signify the play is to the right, and "north" and/or "east" would signify the play is called to the left. The quarterback simply calls the play and direction twice and then issues his cadence. This is an effective and efficient way to get the plays into the remaining five players while keeping the concept well coded from the defense. Any call can be made to signify left or right; it is whatever makes most sense to the players. These left and right indicators can be changed throughout the season or even from one half of the game to the next to keep the defense off balance. The only limit to these calls is the capacity of the athletes to remember them. Time must be taken in the off-season to really drill these concepts and create a profile of each play. Usually, two or three code words for screens and runs are necessary to keep these plays well disguised. Generally, pass plays are easier to disguise, and so one or two words is usually enough.

The snap count that the quarterback uses is very simple. The quarterback will communicate the play and direction and then simply say, "Set, go." The air raid offense is based upon the principles of speed and simplicity, and so only one snap count is used. The offense is able to do this because there is more than one tempo. When the offense wants to go fast, then the "Set, go" cadence will be used, and the offense simply snaps the ball. If there is a concern that the defense might be picking up on this and timing the snap, then the offense will use a version of the check-with-me tempo known as "freeze tempo." The quarterback calls out a play and direction but also makes a call that was predetermined in practice that week to mean that the ball should not be snapped and no one should move. If this signal is used, then the offense just stays still, and the defense will many times jump offside. When this system is used, the defense will usually realize that all plays are on "Set, go" but there is no way of discerning when the offense will actually snap the ball and when they are freezing the defense. This tactic protects the single snap count concept and allows the offense to move quickly and simply down the field.

Tagging Routes

The air raid offense is designed to be a very simple offense for athletes to learn and remember. The ability to alter routes inside of a concept is known as tagging. For example, if the coach wished to add the slant route to X-receiver inside a specific pass concept, this is easily accomplished by flashing a hand signal that signifies the coach is speaking to the X-receiver (Figure 6-4). The signaling coach will then signal what route he wants the player to run. An example might be a slant route, which is accomplished with a karate chop motion with the right hand (Figure 6-5). This system allows the coach to change the routes inside the concept almost limitlessly without being forced to add new pass plays. The tagging potential of the no-huddle system keeps the entire offensive package small yet very versatile.

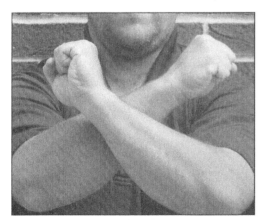

Figure 6-4. X-receiver hand signal

Figure 6-5. Slant route hand signal

Conclusion

The air raid offense is a potent system of plays and schemes that forces defense to adjust and prepare for each week. This style of play is very difficult for defensive coaches and players to simulate in practice. The addition of a no-huddle tempo makes the simulation of this offense even more difficult each week when preparing for it. The key for the offense is to produce a simple system of signaling in plays by hand signal so that athletes on the field can move quickly into position and understand their assignments. The hand signal method makes a common connection in the athletes' minds, and so they are more likely to remember their plays and assignments. In addition, the athletes can easily be given ownership of the signals by enabling them to have a hand in helping to construct them. This approach often leads to a greater degree of pride in the system and a greater degree of determination in remembering the signals.

7

Run Plays

The air raid offense is certainly a pass first style of offensive football. However, the run game in the air raid offense is still very critical to the overall success of the offense. Many defenses prefer to drop multiple defenders into complex coverage alignments when defending an air raid football team. Possessing the ability to run the ball effectively prevents the defense from dropping multiple defenders into coverage. If the defense's strategy is to take away the pass game, the run game must be effective. Keeping a solid balance between the two will keep the defense guessing. The ability to run the ball successfully will take effort from all 11 men on the field. The offensive linemen need to be sure they are blocking their assignment correctly and communicating among one another. The quarterback and ballcarrier must be sure that the timing is exactly where it needs to be and that the exchange is flawless. As easy as this may seem, it needs to be practiced to the point of exhaustion to ensure that no fumbles take place on the exchange. Finally, the players in the receiving corps need to be excellent downfield blockers. The proper execution of blocking by receivers can spring a good gain into a touchdown. The receivers need to take as much pride in blocking as they do in route running. A good starting point is to have a base run game that is simple to teach and to execute. A great deal of time is spent throwing the ball during practice times, so the run game must be efficient, but the number of concepts must be kept to a minimum. Many air raid teams make the decision to keep the offense simple and rely on only two blocking schemes: zone and gap. Two zone schemes and two gap schemes are most commonly utilized in the offense. The offense's base and most called running play is the inside zone, which is coded as Arizona in the no-huddle nomenclature. This play allows the running back to be creative while limiting the amount of plays for the linemen to memorize.

Arizona

The inside zone is a base play for many spread offense–based football teams around the world. The play is effective because it allows the T-back to have the ability to hit the open hole wherever it appears on the line of scrimmage. It is also effective because the offensive linemen apply rules to the defenders in front of them and then block that rule. It is not the responsibility of the offensive linemen to make a hole open at a specific location. This allows the offensive linemen to get off the ball more quickly and attack the defender across from them more aggressively. The offensive linemen must identify if they are covered by a first-level defender playside, covered backside, or uncovered. These three types of coverages will allow the offensive linemen to determine what sort of aiming point and footwork they should be using. These rules were put in place in order to give the offensive linemen the greatest opportunity to create double-teams at the point of attack as possible.

If Arizona is called to the right side of the formation, then the offensive lineman will begin assessing the defender across from them to determine if he is covering them playside or backside or if they have been left uncovered. If an offensive lineman finds himself with a defender head up or lined up in his playside gap, then he will consider himself covered playside. If covered playside, the offensive lineman will execute a hard 45-degree angle step and aim for the defender's outside armpit. If an offensive lineman is covered by a defender in his backside gap away from the call, then he will consider himself covered backside. This will necessitate that the offensive lineman will simply pick his playside foot up and put it right back down without stepping, while at the same time punching with his backside hand into the playside number of the defender covering him backside.

This technique will allow the lineman that is covered backside to slow the upfield rush of the first-level defender while the next lineman inside will be executing a covered playside technique. This will result in a combination block or double-team with both offensive linemen driving the defensive lineman backward and watching for a linebacker or other second-level defender to appear. When a second-level defender appears, the double-team will disengage, and one of the two offensive linemen will come off to execute a block on that defender. If an offensive lineman is completely uncovered with no first-level defender around him, then he will step flat down the line of scrimmage and zone to the first defender that appears in his playside gap. The backside tackle is always considered uncovered because the quarterback will be reading his C gap defender. Therefore, the backside tackle can work to help the backside guard whenever Arizona is called away from him.

The offensive linemen must be prepared to block Arizona versus any kind of defensive front. If Arizona is called to the right and a 3 technique defender is on that side (Figure 7-1), then the playside guard and tackle will be considered covered playside, and they will execute 45-degree angle steps and try to reach the outside armpit of their defender while driving him off the line of scrimmage. The center is covered backside by the 1 technique defender, which also make the backside guard covered playside. The center needs to punch left to help create a double-team with the guard, and then work his way to the second-level defender while the guard attempts to overtake the defender. The backside tackle, by rule, is always uncovered, so he will work his way to a second-level defender. This leaves the backside 5 technique as the read man. If the end crashes and chases the play, the quarterback will keep the ball and run to the voided area. If the defensive end stays home, then the quarterback gives to the tailback. The T-back is coached to aim for the inside leg of the playside guard and proceed "slow to and fast through the hole," meaning the back should be patient to the line looking for the hole to open up then accelerate through the open hole.

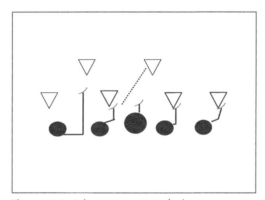

Figure 7-1. Arizona to a 3 technique

The T-back is looking for three different lanes to run through, including the B gap playside, bouncing the play to the outside if containment is not there, or making a cut back if the defender overpursues. These rules stay consistent even if the 3 technique were to be to the backside of the play (Figure 7-2). In this case, the playside guard and center would be making a combo block to the second-level defender and the T-back should theoretically be able to force the ball into the playside B gap. If the Arizona play is called into an odd front such as a 3-2 defense (Figure 7-3), the guards would both be uncovered and follow their rules accordingly. Many teams are also utilizing the 30 stack or 3-3 defense in an attempt to confuse the blocking scheme for the inside zone play. The stack structure is not a problem, and the rules proceed exactly the same as in blocking any other odd front defense (Figure 7-4).

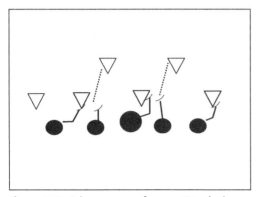

Figure 7-2. Arizona away from a 3 technique

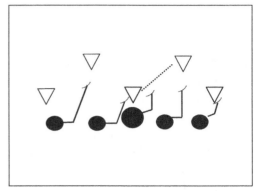

Figure 7-3. Arizona vs. an odd front defense

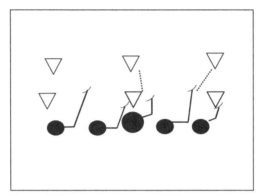

Figure 7-4. Arizona vs. an odd front stack defense

The inside zone or Arizona play is a very versatile play to incorporate into the air raid offense. The spread formations used by the offense pulls defenders out of the box and also allows the offense to run the play from multiple personnel groups and formations. Motion can also be utilized with receivers changing the structure of the defense to make the angles better up front for the offensive linemen. The inside zone can also be packaged with a pitchback or perimeter screens. As long as the offensive linemen grasp the nuances of the covered playside, covered backside, and uncovered rules, and the quarterback and T-back execute their paths and reads correctly the inside zone can be a lethal play that can be run from goal line to goal line from almost any structure.

Oakland

Oakland is the air raid offense's outside zone play. The outside zone is a great complement to the inside zone play because it looks very similar when the ball is first snapped. The Oakland or outside zone play can be run by the T-back or by a motioning receiver in a sort of jet sweep action. The aiming point of the ballcarrier is one yard outside the tight end (or one yard outside where a tight end would line up if a tight end is not in the game). The goal of the play is to get the ball on the perimeter when teams are aggressively attempting to fill holes to stop the inside zone play. The offensive linemen will once again be blocking a rule in order to run this play.

In the outside zone, the entire offensive line will execute an uncovered block rule with one addendum: they will each execute a bucket step instead of a flat uncovered step that was used in the blocking of the inside zone. The bucket step will require each lineman to step at a slight 45-degree angle backward in order to turn his shoulders toward the playside sideline, and then he will aggressively attempt to reach the outside shoulder of the first defender he encounters. If there is no first-level defender, then he will run to the second-level defender on the track they initiated and block his outside shoulder. This is done to cut off defensive pursuit angles and force the ballcarrier onto the perimeter. The key block is by the offensive tackle at the point of attack (Figure 7-5). The tackle must reach the 5 technique so the ballcarrier can reach the edge of the defense. If the offense has trouble accomplishing this block, then a tight end, who may be more athletic and able to reach the 9 technique defender, can be inserted into the game (Figure 7-6). If the tight end is in the game and the defense reduces the 9 technique defender down into a 7 technique, then the tight end will step inside and make sure the defender is overtaken by the offensive tackle and then work the second level.

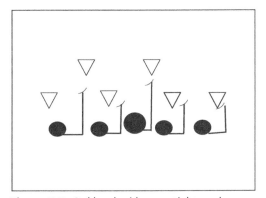
Figure 7-5. Oakland without a tight end

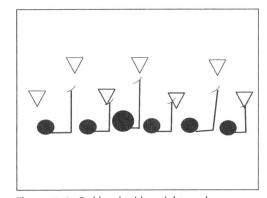
Figure 7-6. Oakland with a tight end

The outside zone is a great play to get the ball to the perimeter and can be run with a variety of formation structures and ballcarriers. The key strategic coaching point however is that the outside zone must be married to the inside zone concept. If a football team is very successful at running the inside zone and is making a lot of yards against a defense, then the outside zone is a great complement play to attack the defense when they are filling interior gaps. If the inside zone is not a large part of the rushing attack for a particular team, then the outside zone is probably not needed.

Giants

Giants is the air raid offense's counter trey run play and has been a very productive play in the offense. The Giants play is used to attack a wide variety of defensive structures and can be utilized regardless of the defense's adjustments. The playside tackle, guard, and center all block down one gap while the backside guard pulls and traps the last man on the line of scrimmage, and the backside tackle pulls up through the hole and lead blocks (Figure 7-7). The play has a natural counter action, as the T-back appears as if the back is going to run the ball the opposite direction of the play by taking a false step before running back to the playside. This extra step also enables the T-back to time up the blocking lanes better by allowing the pulling linemen to complete their assignments. The blocking angles work best when the play is run toward a 3 technique defender (Figure 7-8), but this play is equally useful against odd man fronts that are commonly used by defenses (Figure 7-9).

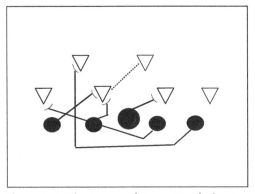

Figure 7-7. Giants away from a 3 technique

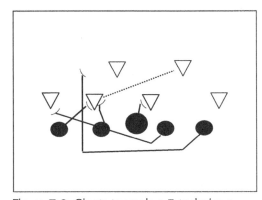

Figure 7-8. Giants towards a 3 technique

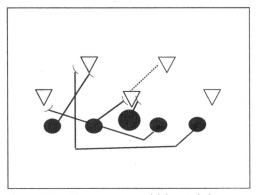

Figure 7-9. Giants vs. an odd front defense

The Giants play is a versatile way to attack modern defenses. The quarterback can either read the backside 5 technique if he is a great running threat, or a tight end or second running back can be inserted into the offensive formation to block the 5 technique. This play marries up well with the scheme of utilizing so much zone blocking. The air raid utilizes a great deal of zone concepts in the run game, so the Giants concept allows the offense to feature the more traditional gap scheme of blocking that generates more power and stops many of the commonly held defensive countermeasures to stopping the zone running game such as squeeze/scrape tactics. In addition, the Giants concept serves as a true character play for the air raid offense by infusing a play with built-in toughness designed to generate yards between the tackles.

Pittsburgh

Pittsburgh is the power run play in the air raid offense. This concept is utilized mainly against odd front defenses when run from a one-back set. The playside tackle will base block the 5 technique, and the playside guard and center will block on to down while the backside guard pulls around and blocks the first second-level defender playside and the backside tackle checks the inside gap and then blocks the backside 5 technique (Figure 7-10). This play is utilized to attack the bubble over the guards that many odd front teams create when they play fewer defenders in the box. The quarterback is not required to read anything and the T-back simply inside steps toward the quarterback and then runs downhill following the pulling guard. This play is a no-finesse way to attack defensive fronts that are designed to stop the complexity of the air raid passing attack.

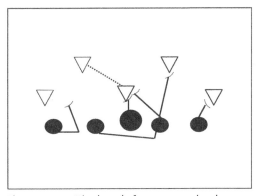

Figure 7-10. Pittsburgh from a one-back set

The Pittsburgh concept can also be run against an even front if a lead blocker is inserted by formation. When the air raid offense features a second back in the backfield, that back can kick out the playside 5 techniques and allow the playside tackle to double-team back with the playside guard. The result is a more traditional looking power play that creates even more leverage at the point of attack (Figure 7-11). The Pittsburgh concept is not used as often as the Giants or Arizona concepts, but it is a great way to generate power and create angles on a defense and give defensive coordinators another concept to stop when facing the air raid offense.

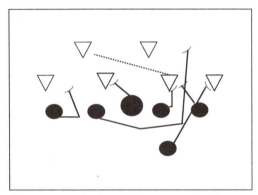

Figure 7-11. Pittsburgh from a two-back set

Denver

The Denver concept is the code name for the dart play. This concept is designed to give the offense another way to run the ball behind lead blockers from a one-back structure. The Denver concept is often called against an even front defense. The playside tackle blocks out while the playside guard blocks on to down. This technique requires the playside guard to block the first level defender wherever he lines up. The center and backside guard will block on to down, and the backside tackle will pull and lead through the first open gap to the playside. When the Denver concept is run toward a 3 technique defender, it is necessary for the backside tackle to pull up through the A gap, and so the play will be an interior run play (Figure 7-12). However, if the play is called toward a 1 technique or nose tackle defender, then the backside tackle will have more room to pull and likely will take his path through the B gap and make the play more of an off-tackle type of play (Figure 7-13).

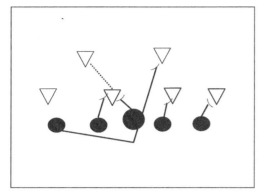 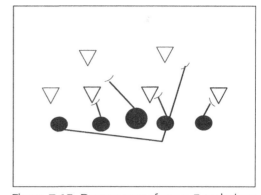

Figure 7-12. Denver toward a 3 technique   Figure 7-13. Denver away from a 3 technique

The Denver concept is designed to look like the Arizona concept with the exception that Denver will have a lead blocker. The most traditional way to run this concept is with the quarterback reading the backside 5 technique just as he does on Arizona. The quarterback can also run this play with a T-back being used to fake across his face and then block the 5 technique. This concept can also feature tight ends or T-backs being used to block the read key in a manner similar to that discussed in the Giants concept section. The Denver concept is another gap scheme run play that has serious similarities to the zone schemes that the offense also utilizes on many plays. The Denver concept then becomes a very simple yet very versatile way to run the ball against modern defenses.

Conclusion

An effective running game is vital for the overall success of an air raid offense. The air raid is an obvious pass first system that will force the defense to focus on stopping the pass game. The ability to take advantage of a defense that has prepared all week for a passing attack is pivotal to overall success. Many defenses will distort their basic packages to stop the advanced passing attack of the air raid offense, and will, therefore, be unable to remain structurally sound against the run game. These concepts are simple to teach and require very little maintenance practice time throughout the season to keep the athletes well-versed in running them. Therefore, these concepts allow an air raid offense to attack and dominate defenses that have made major systemic changes in order to prepare for the passing attack that they expect to face. It is essential that an air raid offense feature simple yet effective run plays to take advantage of the stress that the passing game places on a defense.

8

Screen Plays

It is essential when running the air raid offense, or any spread offense–based system for that matter, that screens are a highly integrated part of the offense. These plays offer not just a way to combat overly aggressive defense, but they also allow the play caller to attack a wide variety of defensive techniques. Screens allow the offense to attack defensive linemen, linebackers, as well as secondary defenders. Each screen is designed to take advantage of a specific defender's technique and style. It is essential that time is set aside each day to work on the timing and technique of these intricate and highly valuable types of plays.

The two main types of screens in the air raid offense are known as fast screens and slow screens. Fast screens are screens that primarily involve the receivers and backs and really require no complex movements by the offensive linemen. These screens, coded as Ducks for the purpose of no-huddle structure, simply required the offensive linemen to full line slide protect in the direction of the screen call when it was a Ducks play. Ducks screens are primarily used to attack zone coverages and as an attempt to punish defenses for playing too soft or not covering all the skilled players on the offensive unit. The Ducks screens quickly become a staple of the offense and are some of the most-called-upon tools in the air raid offense tool bag. The slow screens, coded as Oregon in the no-huddle structure, required extensive use of the entire offensive line and were generally considered to be involving the entire team. The Oregon screens generally are utilized to combat teams that prefer to bring sophisticated pressure packages into games and blitz an air raid offense. These screens allow the defense time to commit to the blitz and then punish them by placing a skilled player into that blitz late with blockers in front. The Oregon screens were called less often, but offered a greater chance of large chunks of offensive yardage to be picked up with each play.

Ducks Screens

The Ducks screens have evolved into a major part of the air raid offense. These plays are almost more of a quick passing package than they are screens, but because there is blocking down the field, almost exclusively by skilled players, they are still categorized as screens. The first play in the Ducks package is the Ducks 1 or bubble screen (Figure 8-1). This play is a basic concept in the air raid offense designed to attack teams that do not cover down all the eligible receivers that are lined up away from the offensive linemen. The goal is to throw the ball quickly to a player who has above-average speed and simply allow him to make plays with the ball in his hands in space with blockers in front. The offensive line simply zones toward the call. The outside receiver blocks the #1 defender from the sideline, and the next receiver inside, if there is one, will block the #2 defender. This play is only thrown if either the #2 or #3 receiver is uncovered or is being leveraged from a distance by a defender. Recently, some teams have dropped the traditional bubble route path because of the amount of repetitions required to perfect this skills set. Instead, the receiver is coached to simply backpedal away from the quarterback with his chest pointing back at the ball. The quarterback is then able to make a simple chest-to-chest pass that has a much higher probability of success. In 2012, Nation Ford's quarterbacks hit the receiver with the ball 100 percent of the time. Not all of these plays were catches, but over 95 percent of them, in fact, were. This high degree of success makes the Ducks 1 or bubble screen one of the most potent plays in the air raid arsenal and a play that can be called with confidence all over the football field.

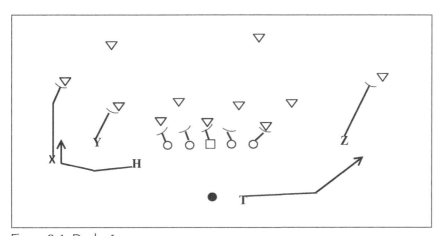

Figure 8-1. Ducks 1

The second screen in the Ducks package is the Ducks 2 or hitch screen. This screen calls for the #1 receiver to execute two steps up the field and then retrace his steps back to his original starting point to catch the football. The #2 receiver will block the force defender over him, and the T-back will execute a kickout block on the #1 defender (Figure 8-2). The offensive linemen's role is still just to zone toward the call. This screen can also be run from a 3x1 alignment. If Ducks 2 is called from trips, then the #1 and #2 receivers assignments stay the same, but instead of the T-back blocking the #1 defender, it is accomplished by the #3 receiver. This play is highly effective to both the wide and short sides of the field, but it can be best utilized into a boundary setting. Many defenses will attempt to cheat the safety toward the wide side of the field, and so there are great blocking angles on the remaining defenders to the boundary side of the field.

The third screen in the Ducks concept is the swing screen to the T-back known as Ducks 3 (Figure 8-3). Ducks 3 is simply a form of a sweep play but is a pass instead of

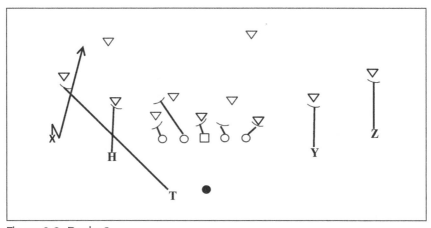

Figure 8-2. Ducks 2

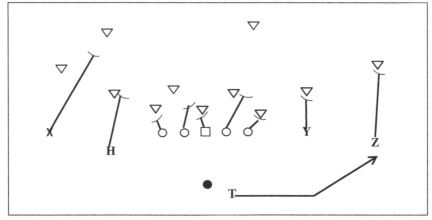

Figure 8-3. Ducks 3

a run play. The quarterback opens his hips and throws to the swinging T-back as quickly as possible. The receivers are charged with blocking the defender in front of them and the offensive linemen again just zone to the call. This play is a great way to get the ball into a great playmaker's hands quickly and also helps to beat teams that attempt to send pressure against the quarterback with a delayed blitz.

Jokers

The Ducks screens have evolved into a large part of the offensive success of air raid teams, and so defenses are attempting to get closer contact to receivers and prevent these kinds of quick-rhythm and high-probability-of-success throws. The offenses' natural response to this is to have play-action passes built into the Ducks package that take advantage of overly aggressive defenders trying to jump the screens. These play-action passes are referred to as jokers. It is important to note that a coach must ensure that a team is actually identifying and attempting to overplay the Ducks screens before the jokers are called. Oftentimes, it is in the second half when teams start doing this, and the joker calls become a more integral part of the game plan of attack.

The first joker would be coded as Ducks 1 joker, for which the same Ducks hand signal would be used, and then a tag would be added to the call that tells the offensive linemen not to go downfield and the receivers to execute the prearranged joker off that screen. In the case of Ducks 1 joker, the #3 receiver would still run a bubble route and the quarterback would pump fake him the football. The #2 receiver would then execute a short post route at a depth of five yards, attempting to work into the middle of the field. The #1 receiver would execute a deep post route at 10 yards and attempt to get behind the safety (Figure 8-4). This concept allows the offense to target the middle linebacker and the downhill hash safety, as they are the players most likely to stop the Ducks 1 screen. If the defense recognizes the play is a joker, then the quarterback can dump the ball back down to the bubble route as his outlet throw.

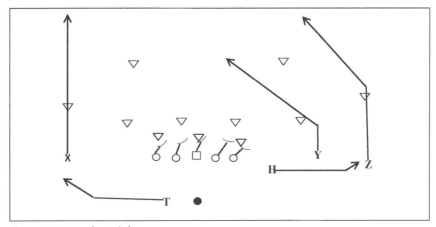

Figure 8-4. Ducks 1 joker

The second joker is Ducks 2 joker. This joker comes off the Ducks 2 or hitch screen action of the offense. The #1 receiver still fakes the Ducks 2 screen action and serves as an outlet throw for the quarterback if something goes wrong with the joker. The #2 receiver will still block the #2 defender. The athlete responsible for the kickout block on the #1 defender—the #3 receiver in a 3x1 alignment, or the T-back in a 2x2 alignment—will then execute a rail route (Figure 8-5). The athlete will simply attack the #1 defender, and once he gets within three steps of him, the receiver or T-back will turn up and sprint down the sideline. The nature of this play is very difficult for defenders to handle because it looks to them like the Ducks 2 screen is being run exactly as before, and they are often coming downhill hard to stop it and miss the athlete turning up on the rail route. The Ducks 2 joker play can also be run with a receiver motioning across the formation (Figure 8-6). This type of motion is used to run the regular Ducks 2 screen, and so the motioning receiver's action looks just like a kickout block until it is too late for the defense to react. The joker plays serve as a useful tool to keep the effectiveness of the Ducks screens going against modern zone defenses.

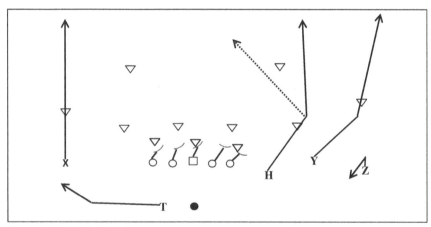

Figure 8-5. Ducks 2 joker

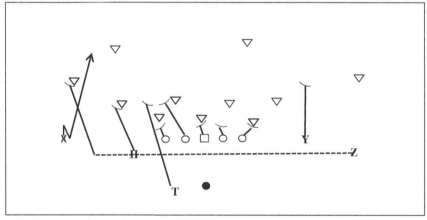

Figure 8-6. Ducks 2 joker with Z motion

Oregon Screens

The Oregon screens are the air raid offense's slow screens (or screens) that allow the defense to bring pressure and then attack voids left in the defense. These screens are all thrown behind the line of scrimmage, and all of them involve significant amounts of blocking downfield by members of the offensive line. These plays are more practice-time-intensive than the Ducks screens. The Ducks screens basically involved one block by the entire offensive line in that they only had to zone block toward the offensive call. The Oregon screens require more complex sets of skills and techniques. For the purpose of explanation, the following blocking techniques will assume that Oregon 1 is called to the right and Oregon 2 and 3 are called to the offense's left. In the interest of simplicity, all of these screens are diagramed from a 2x2 formational structure. However, they can be run from a wide variety of formations and motion sets in reality.

Oregon 1 is a double screen involving the T-back and one of the outside receivers (in this case, the X-receiver). This screen is designed to attack a strong C gap defender that is very difficult for the offense to block on pass plays consistently. The right tackle will execute a rip technique on the first defender outside of him and escape for width to run the alley and block any second- or third-level force defender attempting to run the alley and stop the play. The right guard will execute the same rip release and then block the first second-level defender that he encounters while running at a 45-degree angle from the line of scrimmage. The center, left guard, and left tackle will all execute a rocket screen back to the left of the offense's original position. The left tackle will drop two steps to invite upfield movement by the defensive end, club him past to the outside, and then execute a kickout block on the #2 defender. The tackle must work flat back down the line of scrimmage for the play to be effective. The left guard will work away from the line of scrimmage, after a quick punch to slow his rusher, and attack the first second- or third-level defender to attempt to cross his face. The center will also quick punch a defensive lineman and then release to block the first second- or third-level defender to attempt to cross his face. The #1 receiver to the right will block the #1 defender. The #2 receiver, oftentimes the Y-receiver by alignment, will execute a crack block on the first defender inside to allow the right tackle a clear path to run the alley. The T-back executes a swing route and attempts to get width. The #1 receiver on the left side of the formation executes two vertical steps, retraces his steps, and comes flat back toward the offensive linemen at a depth of one yard behind the line of scrimmage. The #2 receiver to the left side executes a kickout block on the #1 defender. The quarterback's assignment is to take a three-step drop and place his eyes on the C gap defender to the right side. If this defender attacks the quarterback, then he will throw the ball to the swinging T-back as that side of the defense is now outflanked. If the C gap defender peels off to take the T-back in coverage, then the quarterback will flip his hips and throw to the X-receiver coming back inside on a rocket screen (Figure 8-7). The key to this play is that the quarterback must be a good salesman in dropping back and showing pass. He must also quickly deliver the ball to either the T-back or X-receiver as soon as he identifies the action of the C gap defender. If that defender freezes, he is coached to throw the ball to the T-back immediately. A key coaching point is that the X-receiver must stay behind the line of scrimmage to avoid a penalty for having blockers downfield on a passing play.

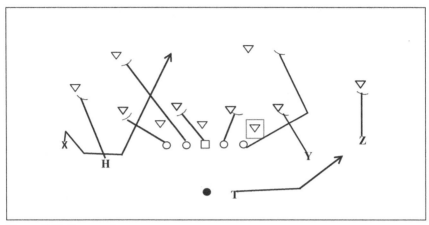

Figure 8-7. Oregon 1

The Oregon 2 screen is the air raid offense's slip screen to the T-back. This particular screen makes things simple for the receivers. All four receivers are coached to run the four-verticals play and run defenders off with them when Oregon 2 is called. The offensive tackles are assigned the role of fan blocking the C gap defenders and pushing them wide to avoid collisions with the T-back. The left guard blocks for a single count and executes a kickout block on the #2 defender is the playside. The center and right guard also execute their block for a single count, and then work for width at a 45-degree angle to block the first second-level defenders that attempt to cross their face. The T-back always starts on the opposite side of the ball (in this case, the right side of the formation). The T-back executes a fake over the ball and then settles behind the left guard. The quarterback immediately begins dropping back when he receives the snap and dumps a short touch pass the T-back over any rushing player's head as soon as he sees the T-back turn to face him (Figure 8-8). This screen is designed to attack the middle of defenses that get upfield to rush the quarterback. Many teams will send edge rushers wide to force the quarterback to step up into pressure. This screen takes advantage of that technique and leaves the defense vulnerable to dealing with the T-back in space once he has the ball in his hands.

The third and final screen in the Oregon package is the rocket screen to the outside receiver (Figure 8-9). This screen is a great way to get the ball on the perimeter to the offense's best players very quickly. The purpose of the screen is to get the ball away from the pocket when overload blitzes are being brought by the defense. Sometimes, teams will bring twist stunts and other pressures that the offense has trouble identifying quickly enough to protect against. The presence of the Oregon 3 (or rocket screen) in the offense forces defensive coordinators to account for this dimension before dialing up their favorite blitz.

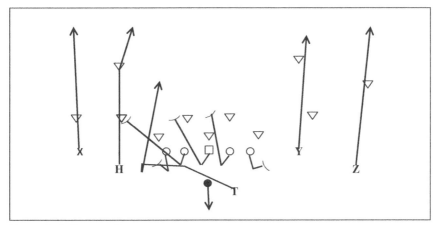

Figure 8-8. Oregon 2

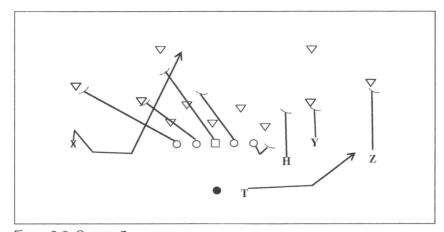

Figure 8-9. Oregon 3

The offensive linemen have very similar rules as to the Oregon 1 screen. The left tackle will drop two steps to invite upfield movement by the defensive end, club him past to the outside, and then execute a kickout block on the #2 defender. The tackle must work flat back down the line of scrimmage for the play to be effective. The left guard will work away from the line of scrimmage, after a quick punch to slow his rusher, and attack the first second- or third-level defender to attempt to cross his face. The center will also quick punch a defensive lineman and then release to block the first second- or third-level defender to attempt to cross his face. The right guard will check the backside A gap for quick penetration, and then also execute a path on a 45-degree angle, looking for second- and third-level defenders. The right tackle will block solid on the defensive end to prevent that defender from getting a clean release to hit the quarterback from the blind side. The backside receivers will run off their defenders. The #1 receiver on the left side of the formation executes two vertical steps, retraces his steps, and comes flat back toward the offensive linemen at a depth of one yard behind the line of scrimmage. The #2 receiver to the left side executes a kickout block on the #1 defender. The quarterback must hold the ball and backpedal as long as possible to invite a rush toward him and then flick the ball over the rushers' heads with touch. This throw must be practiced often for the quarterback to become proficient at it. The throw requires a great deal of wrist action, and the ball must be kept high at all times.

Conclusion

Screens are an integral part of the success of any spread offense. These screens allow the offense to attack basic types of zone coverage through the use of the Ducks package and also attack zone pressures and man pressure packages with the Oregon screens. These screens are the most time-intensive part of implementing the air raid offense. A specific time period must be set aside each day to work on these sorts of plays in the practice plan (see Chapter 4). It is necessary to set up an alternation schedule of Ducks and Oregon screens for the week. Not all the screens have to be run each day, but they should each be worked into the practice plan at least twice each week. Obviously, some screens may not be a large part of the game plan, but if these plays are going to be run on game nights then they must be practiced. The timing required to get all 11 athletes into the right place at the right time requires that all 11 players practice the screens together during the assigned time each day. These plays offer the offense the opportunity to generate a very high proportion of completions and potentially explosive plays that will seriously alter the defenses' game plan. These plays, when executed correctly, can destroy the plans of a defensive coordinator by attacking when he plays too soft in coverage with the Ducks screens and punishing his defense when he attacks the offense with the Oregon screens. These plays are as vital to the success of the offense as any other aspect of the system and must be practiced regularly and with pride to ensure that the offense gets maximum productivity on their time investment.

9

Air Raid Quick Passing Game

The heart and soul of the air raid offense has always been the quick passing game. The goal of the offense is to throw the ball quickly to receivers who can make big plays after the catch. This philosophy allows the quarterback to get rid of the ball very quickly, and so the protection schemes used by the offensive linemen do not have to be complex. These pass plays may involve a simple read by the quarterback, but the majority of the reads are done pre-snap by simply viewing the defense and making an assessment of where the ball should be thrown. The quarterback is coached to scan the defense pre-snap and make assessments. For example, when the hitch route is involved in the pass concept, then the quarterback will immediately take his eyes to the defender over the hitch route and assess whether or not the hitch route will be open after the snap. This is accomplished by noticing the leverage and depth of the defender over that route. For instance, if the route is called to an outside receiver and the cornerback is lined up with a deep cushion and an outside technique, then the quarterback knows he will throw that hitch route immediately after receiving the snap. Every effort is made for the quarterbacks to "cheat" in the quick passing game and get the ball out quickly without reading defenders. In addition, the quarterback will not even take a drop on these routes. He will simply catch and throw without worrying about finding laces or setting his feet. Every effort is made in these concepts to get the ball to the receiver quickly and let him make plays.

Protection

The protection scheme in the quick passing game is uncomplicated. It is basically a half line slide system with the back inserted at key points along the line of scrimmage for protection. A more in-depth explanation of the protection scheme will be included in Chapter 10.

Houston

The all-hitch concept is coded as Houston in this system of play calling. This play is a simple concept that allows for the quarterback to get high rates of completions. This concept requires all the athletes on the field to execute a six-yard vertical release with their arms pumping to sell the defender deep before breaking the route back to the quarterback and settling at five yards (Figure 9-1). These routes are mirrored regardless of formation. One of the best formations from which to run the Houston concept is an empty set because this formation allows the offense to spread the defense the width of the field and isolate defenders (Figure 9-2). This concept is easy for quarterbacks because it is mirrored or identical across the field and allows the quarterback to pick the best match-up that he sees and get rid of the ball. The quarterback is coached daily in practice to pick his best match-up and throw the ball before the receivers turn back to him. This timing makes this a highly effective concept to throw on almost any down-and-distance and one that leads to high rates of completion and great run-after-the-catch potential.

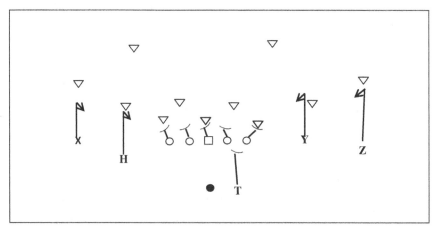

Figure 9-1. Houston concept

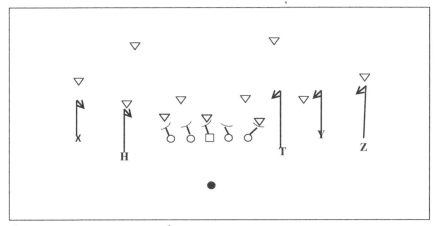

Figure 9-2. Houston concept from an empty set

Huskers

The proliferation of spread offense in recent years has led to more defenses moving away from the traditional one-high-safety or cover 3 family of coverages. Many defenses have moved to a more standard two-high-safety look that allows them to play cover 2 or cover 4. This movement has made the air raid offense adapt its attack methods and some of its concepts. One of the main answers for this proliferation of two-high-safety looks is to attack the corners of the defense. Most corners are taught to play the flat but also be able to get into a quarter of the field to handle deep routes. Modern defenses are asking their corners to perform very complex tasks. The offense's answer to this is to run a concept known as the fade/flat concept, coded as Huskers (Figure 9-3).

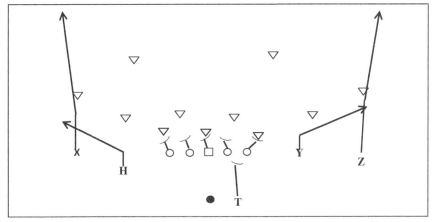

Figure 9-3. Huskers concept

This concept is commonly called out of a 2x2 formation structure to allow the quarterback to mirror read both corners. The basis of the play is very simple in that the receivers are trying to create a high-to-low read on the corner. This concept is only called when the defense is in a two-high-safety structure. The outside receiver will execute an outside release fade route and try to get behind the corner as quickly as possible and stay near the sideline. The inside receiver will drive upfield for three steps and then push for a spot five yards on the sideline. The quarterback is going to read the corner, and if that defender drops deep to defend the fade route, he will immediately execute a throw to the flat route. If the corner stays low in his coverage near the flat, then the quarterback will execute a throw to the outside receiver on the fade route. A key coaching point is that the quarterback must throw the ball with no loft on it. The flat route throw must be executed with a flat trajectory so that the corner cannot close the distance on that receiver. If the quarterback throws the fade route, there is a danger that the safety may make a play on the ball unless it is thrown very flat and hard. Huskers is a very simple way to attack two-high-safety looks and very easy to teach quarterbacks from the youth level through collegiate ranks.

Hawaii

The slant route is a great way to get the ball to athletes very quickly in space while allowing them to run after the catch. The slant route is the basis of a concept known as Hawaii. This concept has route adjustments built in based upon the coverage that the defense plays when it is called. If Hawaii is called and the defense is in a one-high-safety look or cover 3 alignment, then the #1 or outside receiver will run a three-step slant, and the #2 or inside receiver will run a bubble route (Figure 9-4). If Hawaii is called from a 3x1 or trips alignment against this coverage, then the #1 and #2 receivers will both run three-step slant routes, and the inside receiver (#3) will run the bubble route (Figure 9-5). The slant/bubble combination is designed to draw the flat defender or outside linebacker into conflict so that the quarterback can throw the pass off his movement. If the defender works down toward the bubble route, the ball should be thrown to the slant route behind him. If that defender works for depth to cover the slant route, then the ball should be thrown to the bubble route.

The Hawaii concept changes if the coverage is in the two-high-safety families of coverages. In a 2x2 alignment, the outside receiver will still run the three-step slant, but the #2 receiver will run a three-step slant route that stays very "skinny" and attempts to pull the outside linebacker and safety toward the middle of the field (Figure 9-6). The concept of slant routes extends to the 3x1 alignment versus two-high safeties as well. In that 3x1 formation, there will be three slants with the inside two routes both being skinny slant routes (Figure 9-7).

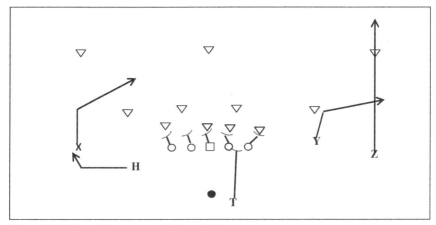

Figure 9-4. Hawaii vs. cover 3 from 2x2

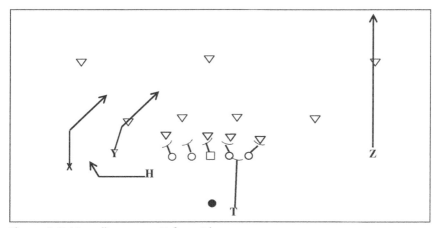

Figure 9-5. Hawaii vs. cover 3 from trips

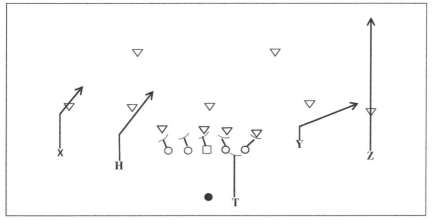

Figure 9-6. Hawaii vs. cover 2 from 2x2

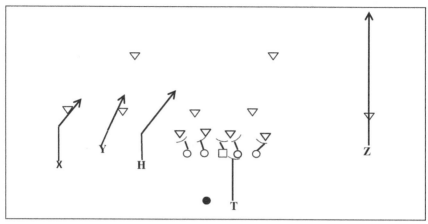

Figure 9-7. Hawaii vs. cover 2 from trips

Hawkeye

The Hawkeye concept is a great way to convert first downs, touchdowns, and most specifically two-point conversions. The Hawkeye concept is an option route by the Y-receiver. The Y-receiver is oftentimes the best big man on the offense. Most air raid teams feature their tight end in this position or an athlete who is very physically strong. At Nation Ford, this athlete is a power forward recruited from the basketball team; he is 6'3" and weighs around 215 pounds. He is an athlete with a great deal of body control, who can execute the route effectively against outside linebackers and strong safeties. The option route that the Y-receiver will execute is a six-yard route. The Y-receiver is instructed to push vertically to six yards, initiate contact with the first defender over him, and then hitch inside, outside, run inside, or run outside as necessary to get open. The route is designed to use the size of the Y-receiver to gain leverage on the flat defender.

The goal of this play is to isolate the Y-receiver and let him work against one defensive player. The #1 receiver to the playside will run an outside release fade route and any other defender on that playside will drag away from the Y-receiver and get to the other side of the field on a shallow route. The first receiver backside will run a 10-yard dig route and any other backside receiver will run a vertical route. The best way to run this play is from a 2x2 empty set with the T-back set just inside the Y receiver (Figure 9-8). This concept allows the Y-receiver to run his route in any direction while the inside and outside defenders are taken away from the Y-receiver's path. A key coaching point is that the quarterback must be coached to stare down the Y-receiver and throw the ball to his open hand as soon as he feels that the Y-receiver is open. The Y-receiver is taught to show his hands to the quarterback if he is going to stop, and show his eyes if he is going to keep running. In this way, the quarterback knows whether or not the Y-receiver is planning to stop on his route or continue running.

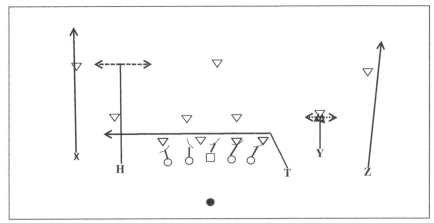

Figure 9-8. Hawkeye concept

Washington

The stick concept, code named "Washington," has been a centerpiece of the air raid offense for several years. This play is a great way to the get the ball to the Y-receiver, but more importantly, it allows the offense to have an answer to almost any coverage family. The Washington concept attacks the bottom low defenders of the defense and attempts to make larger middle and outside linebackers cover athletic football players in space.

The basic premise of the concept, from a 3x1 alignment, is to have the #1 receiver playside execute a mandatory outside release fade route to make the corner turn his hips to the outside. This is a critical coaching point because if the corner's hips are not forced to turn, then he will be in position to drive back inside to attack the #2 receiver's route. The #2 receiver will run three steps upfield, and then roll over his inside foot and sprint into a flat route at a depth of no more than five yards. The #3 receiver, who is usually the Y-receiver, will push on a preferred inside release up to a height of six yards, and then read the coverage over him. If the first defender inside is not attached, then he will turn outside and sit his route down with his hands showing to the quarterback (Figure 9-9). If the defender is attached, or covering down on the Y-receiver, then he will push off and work outside into the next available hole in the defense.

The Washington concept can be executed very well from a 2x2 alignment in addition to the more popular 3x1 structure. If the Y-receiver is in a tight end alignment, then he will take an inside release and execute the stick route (Figure 9-10), and the T-back will provide the flat route component of the concept. The Y-receiver is still trying to push off the first defender inside, who is likely the middle linebacker. The T-back can execute a swing route or flat route based upon what gets him to outflank the flat defender more quickly.

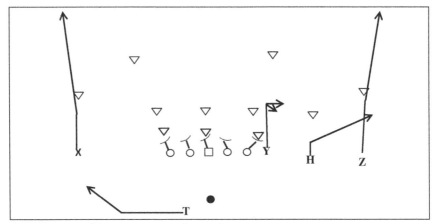
Figure 9-9. Washington concept from trips

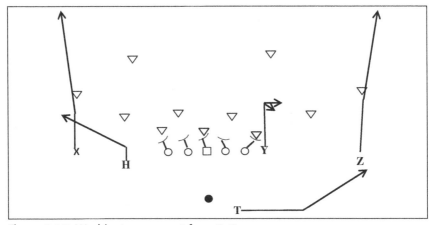
Figure 9-10. Washington concept from 2x2

Hoosiers

The Hoosiers concept is one in which the quarterback can really gain a sense of familiarity with when he needs to get short completions. This play is a byproduct of how well teams run the stick concept (Washington) and so it serves as a great complement to the stick concept in the air raid offense. The snag concept (Hoosiers concept) is one that has at least partial origins in the West Coast offense of Bill Walsh but the idea goes back into the early days of passing concepts. The goal is quite simple, to put one defender in conflict with two athletes. It is very similar to what was done with the Washington concept in terms of putting two quick routes on each side of a low defensive player. In this concept, from a standard 2x2 alignment, the #1 receiver will still run the outside release fade route to take the corner's head and hips away from what is happening inside. The #2 receiver will then run a snag route. This route calls for him to take two steps up the field, then break four steps inside at a 45-degree angle, and finally sit down and face the quarterback with his hands facing back toward the ball. The #3 receiver will execute either a bubble or flat route based upon what is preferred with that particular athlete (Figure 9-11). This play can also be run effectively by lining up or motioning to trips and letting the #3 receiver be a receiver on the line of scrimmage rather than a T-back in the 2x2 alignment (Figure 9-12).

There is a simple way to exchange who runs the snag route and who takes the top off the coverage. This concept is called "Hoosiers switch." The *switch* code word tells the #1 receiver to run the snag route and the #2 receiver to take the deep outside route. This goal is accomplished by the #1 receiver cheating his alignment down and running the same technique, two steps up and four steps in, while the #2 receiver will execute a corner route, breaking at the top of the stem at around 10 to 12 yards (Figure 9-13).

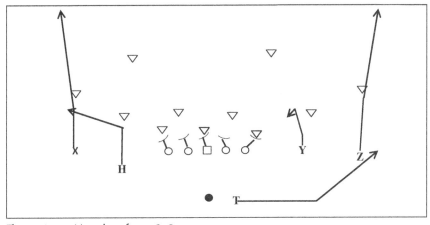

Figure 9-11. Hoosiers from 2x2

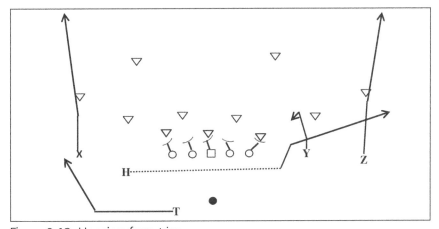

Figure 9-12. Hoosiers from trips

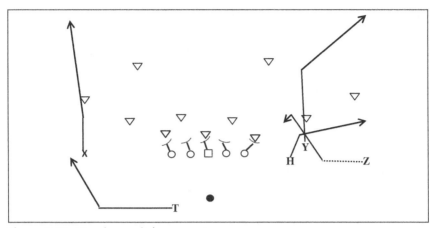

Figure 9-13. Hoosiers switch concept

Ninja

Recent times have seen a push toward combining quick passes with more traditional dropback passes in the spread offense. The University of Wisconsin-Whitewater and the staff at Sacred Heart-Griffin High School in Springfield, Illinois, have done a great job utilizing a system that they call the "hitch-naked concept." This concept has been researched and adapted and the result is a concept known as ninja. This concept is an excellent way to attack defense because it not only features both a quick and dropback pass pattern, but it also moves the launch point of the quarterback. In a 2x2 structure, ninja would be called to the X-receiver on the left. This call tells the X-receiver to run a hitch route automatically unless he sees a press corner technique, which means he would covert the route to a fade route. The rest of the receiver corps is running a flood concept back into the field (Figure 9-14). The same idea holds true if the ninja concept is called from a 3x1 structure in that the X-receiver will have the ninja route and the rest of the team executes a flood concept to the field (Figure 9-15). The offensive linemen are instructed to always full zone slide protect to the ninja call, while the back works away from the quarterback's read and then steps back to pin the defensive end. The quarterback's responsibility is to throw the ninja if it is open immediately every time. If the route is not open, then he will pump fake, roll around the T-back's pin block, and then execute the flood concept.

The ninja concept can be married with a smash concept to the field as well (Figure 9-16). The key is that the quarterback must throw the ninja concept each and every time that it is open and be alert for a conversation on the hitch route to a fade or a slant route. The strategy behind the concept is for the quarterback to have an easy, quick pass open to him every play and, if it is covered, to have an equally simple to execute dropback pass coming open on the wide side of the field. The quarterback must be coached to make his decision about the ninja side of the field quickly, and then move on with his wide side read.

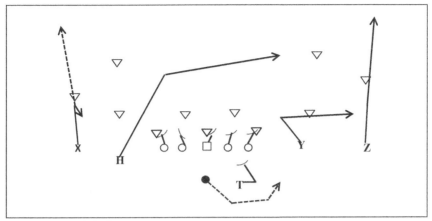

Figure 9-14. Ninja from 2x2

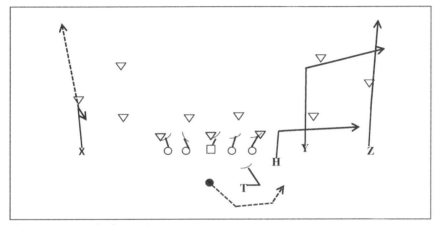

Figure 9-15. Ninja from trips

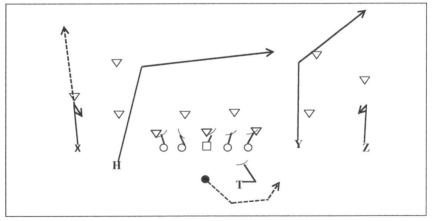

Figure 9-16. Ninja with a smash concept

Conclusion

The quick passing game is the key component to a successful air raid offense. The offense is predicated on getting the ball out of the quarterback's hands quickly and into the hands of skilled players who can score. These plays allow for the offense to strike quickly against multiple defensive coverages without mentally taxing the offensive players. The plays offer a high percentage and variable array of answers to anything that defenses attempt to do to stop the air raid offense. The protection schemes of the offense are very simple, and the system is designed to be simple and play at a very quick pace. Therefore, the quick passing game must be simple to remember and easy to execute. Many more quick passes might be employed, but this portion of the offense must be very dependable, and the athletes on the field must get a high number of repetitions so that they have a lot of confidence when quick passes are called.

10

Air Raid Dropback Passing Game

The heart and soul of the air raid offense has always been the quick passing game, and the goal of the offense is still to throw the ball quickly to receivers who can make big plays after the catch. However, the air raid is a tool that is used for a specific mission and for a specific team type. Most air raid teams are employing the system because they have an abundance of skill players, and they feel that they would lose a traditional slugging match with most superiorly athletic teams. Therefore, it is necessary to score points and too often score them in droves. Many air raid teams will give up yards and points in defense, and most offensive coordinators in this system know that they will not be involved in many 10-6 score type of games. This knowledge lends itself to the need for an air raid offense to have the capacity to strike down the field and inflict optimum damage on its opponents in a very short period of time. This goal is accomplished through the use of an effective dropback passing game.

The quarterback in this system will be operating predominantly from the shotgun. When the quick passing game or three-step passing game is translated to the shotgun, it is necessary to take two steps off the drop to facilitate timing. Therefore, quick passes from the shotgun become one-step catch-and-throw situations. The same thing is done in the dropback passing scheme from the shotgun. If the quarterback is charged with a five-step pass from the shotgun, then he will turn it into a three-step pass. This helps the quarterback to gather his steps more quickly and prepare to deliver the ball quickly. The base philosophy of the offense is still to allow the quarterback to get rid of the ball very quickly, and so the protection schemes used by the offensive linemen do not have to be complex. The quarterback is still coached to scan the defense pre-snap and make assessments. However, in the dropback passing game, he is expected to make actual reads before throwing a pass. The air raid read progression is: peek, 1, 2. This progression includes no actual reads of the defense.

The quarterback is taught to key the movements of defenders, but he is not expected to read them. Asking a quarterback to read defenders is problematic because the offense cannot control where these people move on a given play. The offense cannot control where the defense is going to be during a play. The only thing the offense can control is where the receivers will be during a play. The quarterback will come to the line of scrimmage and peek the deepest route in the concept. If he likes the match-up, then he will throw to the deep route immediately. If he does not like it, his eyes go to his nearest throw or shortest throw on the field, which is his first read. If that read is covered, then he will work to his second read, which is the middle receiver in the concept. The quarterback is never asked to read more than three things in a route concept. He walks to the line pre-snap, reads deep, and then checks shallow to middle and throws the ball. This system of reading keeps things simple and standard for all dropback pass plays. Every effort is made in these concepts to still get the ball to the receiver quickly and let him make plays.

Protection

The air raid offense operates at a very quick pace and gives defense only minimal time to adjust between plays. It is essential that everything done in the offense is accomplished with an eye toward keeping things simple. Therefore, one standard protection scheme is used for both quick and dropback passes. The protection is called by the T-back on every play with a code word that either slides the offensive line to the right or left. The T-back then inserts himself into the open gap on the side of the line where he called the protection. If the back calls the protection to the right, then the right tackle and right guard will take the first two down linemen to that side of the ball, and the T-back will take the linebacker to that side while the rest of the line slides their protection weak and picks up the first three rushers from that side (Figure 10-1).

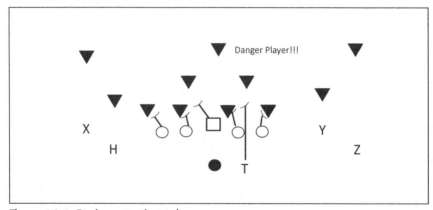

Figure 10-1. Basic protection scheme

The simplicity of this protection scheme holds up regardless of formation. If the T-back were to be out in the formation in an empty set, he would still call the protection, and the offensive line would slide accordingly, with the linebacker to the callside being a hot read for the quarterback. The only time that a quarterback has to be ready to throw hot is if there is an empty set or the defense goes into man coverage with a no-high-safety look. Many defenses are unwilling to take overly aggressive risks with a pass first offense, and so the protection scheme is rarely overwhelmed by an excess of blitzes that would require a hot throw. This system means that no complicated coverage has to be called or checked to, and the linemen get very comfortable knowing who they will block on each and every play. This repetitive protections system makes the quarterback easier to protect and saves valuable time in practice and between plays.

Texas Tech

The base concept of most spread offenses is the four-verticals pass play. This concept gives the air raid offense the ability to strike down the field and attack multiple coverages. The #1 receivers on both sides of the ball in a 2x2 formation run fade routes and try to get behind the deep defender. The #2 receivers will run seam routes two yards outside the hash marks and stay locked into those seams if the coverage is a one-high-safety look (Figure 10-2). If the coverage observed is a two-high-safety look, then the outside receivers will still run fade routes, and the Y-receiver will stay on a locked seam route two yards outside the hash marks, but the H-back will change his seam route into a post route. The H-back is coached to avoid the outside linebacker by any means necessary and then break his route into the open area between the two safeties (Figure 10-3). The T-back is running an option route over the ball at four yards to hold the linebackers. If the linebackers bail into coverage, then the T-back is an easy outlet for the quarterback.

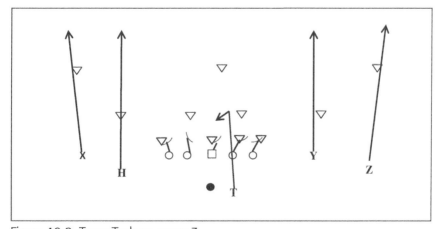

Figure 10-2. Texas Tech vs. cover 3

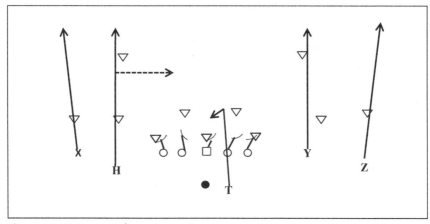

Figure 10-3. Texas Tech vs. cover 4

The Texas Tech concept is an easy play to tag in the air raid offense. One way to tag the route is to run the base concept but tag one of the outside receivers on a comeback route (Figure 10-4). This is an easy way to get corners to back up and then execute easy throws for first downs underneath them. Another easy tag from the Texas Tech concept is to tag "X-under" onto the play and let the X-receiver run underneath the coverage and find an opening on the other side of the ball while the other athletes all keep their base assignments (Figure 10-5). These are two easy ways to make this concept more versatile in attacking a wide variety of defenses. The number of tags off the Texas Tech concept is almost limitless, and so the play can be called versus almost any coverage or front structure that the defense might show.

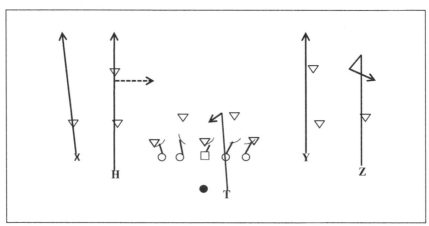

Figure 10-4. Texas Tech comeback tag

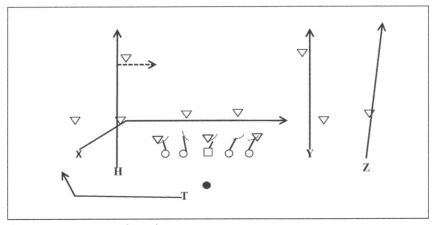

Figure 10-5. Texas Tech under tag

Alabama

The proliferation of spread offenses has led to more defenses utilizing two-high-safety looks in order to stop the easy completions of the four-verticals concept. The natural evolution of this change in defensive structure is for offense to attack the area behind the corners and outside the safeties. A large area of grass is left uncovered, as it is expected that either the corner will bail to that zone or the safety will drift there once the routes are identified that the offense is running. The basis of the smash or Alabama concept is to have the #1 receiver run a short hitch route to hold the corner, and then allow the #2 receiver to execute a corner route behind the corner's position. The hitch route will be a four-yard back to three-yard route, and the corner route will push vertically for 10 yards, head fake to the post route, and then break at a 45-degree angle for the sideline at 22 yards (Figure 10-6).

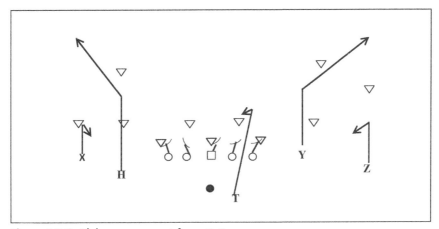

Figure 10-6. Alabama concept from 2x2

The basis of the Alabama concept is to put the corner into a high-to-low bind and make him make a decision quickly. If the corner stays on the hitch, then the #2 receiver should gain the open grass and be open. If, however, the corner bails at the snap of the ball, then the quarterback can throw the ball to the hitch route and get the ball out of his hands quickly. If the concept is run from a 3x1 set, then the #3 receiver will execute a seam route to attack the safety further while the backside #1 receiver will execute a shake corner route to hold the backside safety with all the quarterback reads being maintained (Figure 10-7).

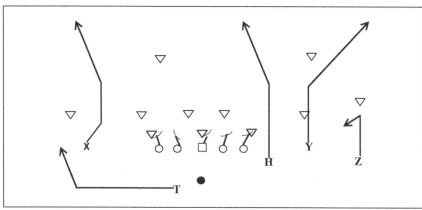

Figure 10-7. Alabama concept from trips

Florida

The Florida or flood concept is designed to attack defenses by placing receivers at three levels on one side of the field. This concept makes the reads for the quarterback very easy, and the ball is usually able to be thrown quickly and on target. This concept can be run from a straight dropback set or, if the quarterback needs to be closer to his target or is an agile runner, from a rollout position. This concept is often run from a 3x1 alignment and calls for the #1 receiver to run an outside release fade route. The goal of the #1 receiver is to attempt to beat the coverage deep down the sideline. The #2 receiver will take a slight inside release and gain ground up to 12 yards before rounding the route off to about 14 yards onto the sideline. This route run by the #2 receiver is often referred to as a sail route. The #3 receiver will take two steps up the field and then run immediately to the flat on a flat route at a depth of no more than four yards. This concept creates an easy read for the quarterback as he is coached to peek the #1 receiver and then work his read back to the flat route and finally to the sail route (Figure 10-8). The backside receiver executes a skinny post route and serves as a "homerun throw" or touchdown-maker for the quarterback, should the coverage attempt to roll toward the 3x1 side of the play. The Florida concept is a great way to get the ball quickly to athletes in space and makes the quarterback's reads very simple. For these reasons, the Florida concept is a mainstay of the air raid offense and is a concept that can be called on almost any down or distance and against almost any coverage structure.

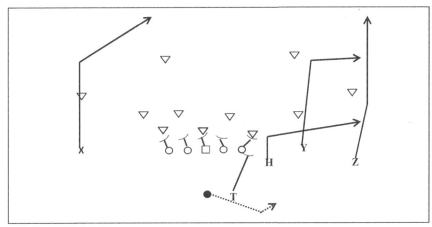

Figure 10-8. Florida concept

Wyoming

A trend is growing toward teams playing two-high-safety looks against the air raid offense. However, some teams still attempt to play some one-high-safety looks or mixed coverages. Therefore, one of the basic concepts inside the air raid offense remains the curl/flat concept. The code name for this concept is Wyoming. The basic premise of the concept is to create a read on the flat or alley defender. The concept is mirrored on both sides of the field so that the same read is created on both alley defenders. The #1 receiver to the callside (in this case, to the right side) will release slightly inside and execute a 14-yard back to 12-yard curl route. If the formation is a 2x2 set, then the T-back will run a swing route underneath the curl route to create a read on the alley defender, while the #2 receiver will execute a tagged route from the sideline designed to attack the weaknesses in the middle of the defense. This tagged route could be a deep seam route (Figure 10-9) or short hitch route (Figure 10-10) based upon what the defense is doing to stop the play.

If the concept is run from a 3x1 set, then the #1 receiver will still execute the curl route, but the #2 receiver will run a five-yard out route, attempting to gain width onto the sideline. The #3 receiver will still be tagged onto a route based upon coverage, and the T-back will swing to the weakside of the formation under the backside curl route being run by the #1 receiver (Figure 10-11). This concept keeps the routes mirrored

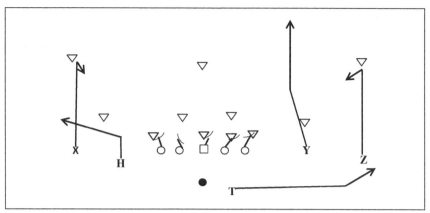

Figure 10-9. Wyoming concept with a seam tag

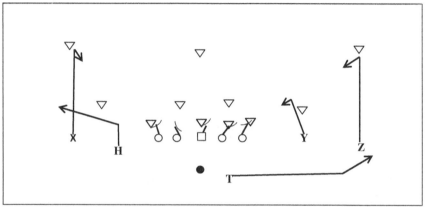

Figure 10-10. Wyoming concept with a hitch tag

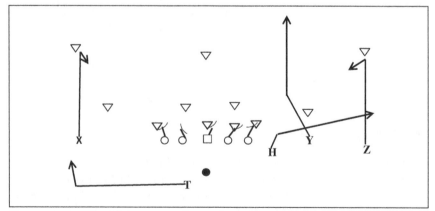

Figure 10-11. Wyoming concept from trips

to both sides so that the quarterback can pick which side he wants to throw the ball to pre-snap. The ability to tag one route inside the concept each time it is run gives the play caller or quarterback (who often calls the tag) the flexibility to find holes inside the coverage and attack them while maintaining the base structure and reads of the original concept.

The play can also be tagged with a shake tag to change the nature of the routes. If Wyoming shake is called, then the #1 receiver will execute a slight inside release and push vertically to 14 yards, but instead of breaking into a curl route he will head fake inside and then execute a corner route (Figure 10-12). All the other receivers still follow the base rules of the Wyoming concept. This tag is a great way to attack cover 2 defenses that attempt to attack the curl routes when they see the inside release of the #1 receiver. The Wyoming shake concept adds another wrinkle into the air raid offense that allows it to attack any coverage once it has been identified.

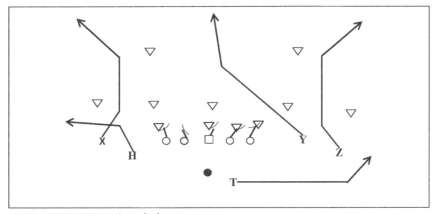

Figure 10-12. Wyoming shake concept

Kansas

One of the staples of any version of the air raid offense is the shallow cross concept, coded as the Kansas concept. The goal of the concept is to create a quick read of the linebackers by running a shallow crossing route underneath them while at the same time running a dig route above them. The read is, therefore, directly in front of the quarterback where he can make quick decisions and deliver the ball with a high rate of accuracy.

The first part of the Kansas call requires the offense to know which player will be running the shallow cross route. A hand signal is given that designates which athlete will run the route. If the concept is called in a 2x2 formation and the Y-receiver is tagged with the shallow cross route, then he will execute the route by running at the heels of the defensive linemen (Figure 10-13). He is allowed to gain as much as five yards of ground up the field once he passes the center. The first receiver on the other side of

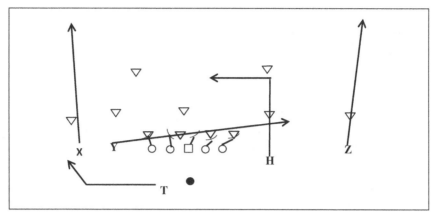

Figure 10-13. Kansas concept

the ball will execute an outside release and run a dig route at 12 yards. The key to this route is that the receiver not get pushed inside. He is coached to take an exaggerated release to the outside so that the man covering him is forced to turn his hips and thereby miss the Y-receiver running the shallow cross route from the other side of the field. The first receiver outside the shallow cross route runs a deep fade route. The first receiver outside the dig route runs a deep post route and attempts to get above any safety on that side of the field. The T-back is coached to check his protection toward the shallow cross route and, if there is no pressure, to attack the flat where the shallow cross route originated from at the snap.

This concept is generally run from a 2x2 alignment and is a very easy read for the quarterback. The quarterback is able to read the deep post and fade routes back to the shallow cross route and finally read the dig route over the middle of the field. This concept is a great way to attack large middle linebackers who are in the game to tackle running backs rather than chase wide receivers. This concept also makes man coverage very difficult with all the crossing receivers and allows the offense to have a built-in pass play against teams that want to blitz from the middle of the field. The Kansas or shallow cross concept can be run from multiple sets or formations by simply applying the base rules. The key is to tag one receiver as the shallow cross route runner, and then the next receiver on the other side of the ball will know to execute the dig route. Everyone else on the field takes their cue from the shallow cross route, and so the concept is very versatile and athletes can play multiple positions on the field and still execute the play. Another popular way that the concept can be run is to use short motion by the Z-receiver and then tag him with the shallow cross route (Figure 10-14). The simple application of the tag system allows this play to be a dynamic and simple way to attack modern defense.

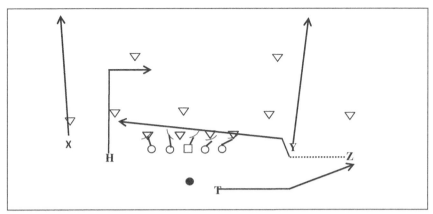

Figure 10-14. Kansas concept with Z short motion

Clemson

The Y-receiver is an integral part of the success of the air raid offense. This athlete is not usually the fastest or even the best all-around receiver on the team, but he is always one of the most versatile athletes in the program. The Y-receiver is asked to do a great deal of blocking, screening, and short route running while not be involved in a lot of the deeper routes on the field. In order to compensate for how often he runs short routes, the Y-cross concept or Clemson concept came along as a way to get him the ball in space away from the larger defenders he usually has to contend with on quick passes. This concept is designed to get the Y-receiver open against smaller defenders and allow him to punish them with his size.

The Y-receiver will execute the deep cross route when he receives the Clemson hand signal from the sideline. He will release inside as if he is running a shallow crossing route, then build vertically to a depth of about 10 yards, he will then break a third time and run at a 45-degree angle, aiming for a spot on the far sideline at 18 yards of depth. It is essential that the Y-receiver do everything possible to avoid contact during this route and maintain eye contact with the quarterback after he reaches 10 yards. The first receiver outside of the Y-receiver will run a fade route that can be converted back to a dig route by hand signals. The first receiver on the other side of ball will execute a five-yard option route and break either inside or outside based upon coverage in an attempt to find an open area. This route helps to hold the alley defender down on that side so that the Y-receiver can gain ground above him and find an opening. The first receiver outside the option route will execute either a fade route or a post route based upon what the quarterback feels is necessary to attack the top of the coverage to keep defenders from jumping the Y-receiver's route (Figure 10-15). The T-back always executes his protection toward the Y-receiver when Clemson is called and will work into the backside flat if no blitz materializes.

The Y-receiver is the principal recipient of the Clemson call, but other athletes can be tagged to run the route if desired. One of the most common ways to achieve the same concept, while getting a faster athlete to run the deep cross route, is to put the Z-receiver into short motion and tag him with the Clemson route and let the Y-receiver take the fade route (Figure 10-16). This has proven to be a good disguise of the route concept and oftentimes allows the Z-receiver to get a clean release and a running start toward his aiming point. The quarterback's reads always take him to the post and fade routes first followed by the option route and finally the deep cross route. However, if the receiver running the deep cross route and the quarterback read an interior linebacker blitz, then the deep cross route can convert immediately into a hot route, and the ball can be delivered to the receiver in space and on the run. The Clemson concept attacks some large grass areas in the defense and creates natural run-after-the-catch opportunities for skilled players.

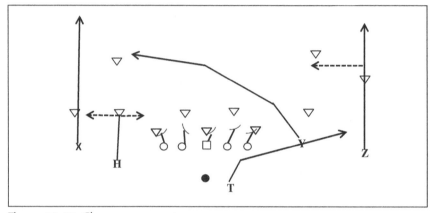

Figure 10-15. Clemson concept

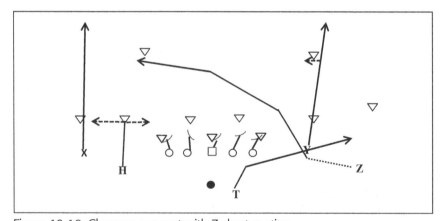

Figure 10-16. Clemson concept with Z short motion

Georgia

The Georgia concept is a hybridization of two existing air raid concepts, which are the mesh concept and the drive concept. There is a constant attempt to limit the number of plays that athletes are asked to remember. In its most basic form, the Georgia concept is, in fact, the drive concept, but it can be easily tagged and adjusted to allow it to conform and include the basic premises of the mesh concept as well.

The basic Georgia concept requires that a receiver be tagged with the Georgia call. The Z-receiver, for example, has been tagged with the Georgia route, and so he will execute a drive route in which he drives across the field, slowly gaining ground to a depth of five yards (Figure 10-17). The drive route is not allowed to stop unless he has passed the backside offensive tackle. The first receiver inside the drive route will execute an outside release, attempting to create a rub for the Z-receiver and work to a depth of 12 yards and then run a dig route back into the middle of the field. The first receiver on the other side of the ball will execute a post route and attempt to get over the top of the safety. The first receiver outside the post route will run a fade route. The T-back is coached to run a swing stop route toward the drive route in order to pull defenders wide away from the play. The quarterback takes his eyes first to the deep post route and then works back to the drive route and finishes his read on the dig route. The quarterback is coached to key the movement of the middle linebacker and use that defender as an extra key as to where he should deliver the football.

When the play is run from a 3x1 formation, the basic rules all still apply. The drive route is almost always tagged to the #2 receiver and that allows the #1 receiver to take the top off the coverage deep (Figure 10-18). The single receiver backside then runs the post route, and the T-back goes through the single receiver side of the line of scrimmage and works back toward the drive route's origin as he would do by rule

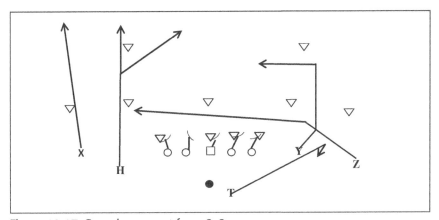

Figure 10-17. Georgia concept from 2x2

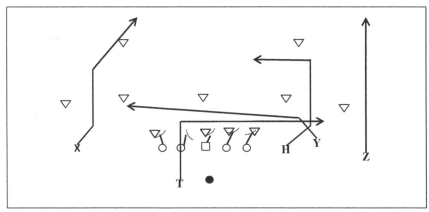

Figure 10-18. Georgia concept from trips

in a 2x2 set. The T-back is required to take his path through the line of scrimmage to discourage teams from blitzes through the weakside of the offensive line in order to get pressure on the quarterback. The T-back must stay underneath the drive route and work for width back into the trips side flat.

The Georgia concept is also a great play to run from a 3x2 or empty set as well (Figure 10-19). In this case, the T-back will just drag underneath the drive route and create a form of a mesh route with the Y-receiver.

The Georgia concept can be transformed into a mesh concept to attack man coverage very easily. The same 2x2 alignment is used, and the Z-receiver is still the drive route runner, but the concept is tagged with a mesh hand signal (Figure 10-20). This hand signal will cause the first receiver on the other side of the ball from the drive route to mesh underneath the drive route. The next receiver backside would then assume the role of the post route. The T-back is allowed to swing freely instead of stopping his route. This tag allows the Georgia concept to have a built-in tag to attack man coverages that might attempt to chase the drive route across the field.

The Georgia concept can be altered further by calling Z "Georgia" from the same 2x2 alignment as previously discussed and then adding both a mesh and a corner route tag (Figure 10-21). This makes the play a cover 2 and man-coverage beater all rolled into one small package. The ability to tag these concepts together has allowed the offense to reduce two or three plays into just one concept, thereby reducing the amount of information that athletes have to remember.

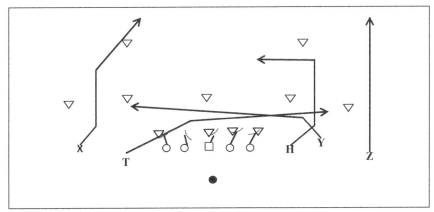

Figure 10-19. Georgia concept from an empty set

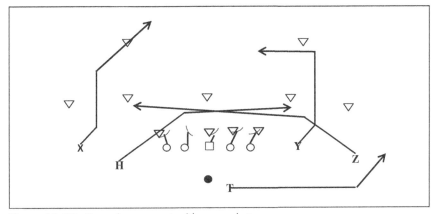

Figure 10-20. Georgia concept with a mesh tag

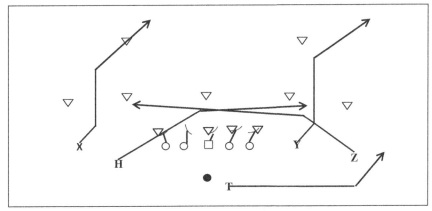

Figure 10-21. Georgia concept with a mesh and corner tag

South Carolina

The South Carolina concept (or Gamecock, as it is called in the no-huddle structure) is a split field read concept. The concept is almost exclusively a 3x1 route structure play designed to create a cover 3 coverage option on one side of the field and a cover 2 or cover 4 read play on the other side of the field. The quarterback is taught to read the one-receiver side first and determine if the coverage allows him to throw the ball there. If that side of the field is not an option, then he works his read back to the three-receiver side of the field. The entire decision-making process is done pre-snap by the quarterback, and he should know where to throw the ball before it is snapped to him by the center.

The one-receiver side will execute a glance post route. The glance route is designed to have the receiver run seven steps vertically and then break into a glance or skinny post that is designed to work up the hash mark and stay out of the middle of the field. The T-back will be aligned to this side, and he will execute a check swing route into the flat. The quarterback is looking for a safety who has overrotated away from this side of the field. If there is no safety help to the inside, then the quarterback will throw to this side as he has a match-up advantage. If there is safety help over the top, then the read goes to the three-receiver side of the concept. The #3 receiver to the trips side will execute a five-yard in route. This route is designed to be run as an outside release to five yards and then break inside to find a hole in the defensive coverage. The #2 receiver will drive inside at a 45-degree angle until he hits a depth of five yards, and then find a hole in coverage to settle down. The #3 receiver will wheel outside the #2 receiver to rub off any man coverage and then build to a depth of 12 yards before breaking back to the inside on a dig route. This structure is designed to hold all the linebackers down while opening a hole behind them for the dig route to run (Figure 10-22).

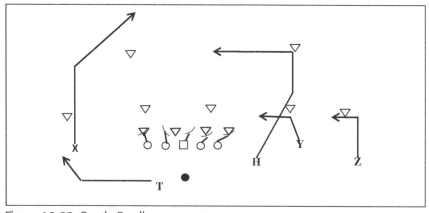

Figure 10-22. South Carolina concept

Conclusion

The air raid offense is a dynamic and multi-faceted system designed to attack defenses across the width and depth of the football field. The ability to throw the ball down the field in the dropback passing game gives the air raid the undeniable ability to stay in games regardless of physical talent disparities. The willingness and desire to attack the defense and stretch them down the field opens up higher completion percentage screens and quick passes along with the air raid running game. While completion percentage is certainly an indicator of success, it is not the most important aspect of the dropback passing game. This component of the offense is designed to take risks, attack defenses, open up the other aspects of the offense, and above all to score points. The dropback passing attack of the air raid offense is the means by which the offense is able to amass large numbers of points and dictate the style of games in its favor.

11

Air Raid Game Planning

Preparation and organization are necessary in order to be successful in the game of football. So much needs to be done each week to get a team ready to play that the workload must be shared. In order to share the workload, it is essential that all the coaches on staff share the vision and share the mission of the program. If the air raid offense is to be successful, then it is necessary to have a group of coaches in place that all support the idea of playing fast, scoring points, and taking risks. Many coaches simply do not feel that this is an effective way to play the game and would prefer a more conventional approach to the game. These coaches certainly have their own style and own motivations, but they should not be on a staff that has committed to running the air raid offense. Therefore, the first component of game planning the air raid offense is to select good coaches who are compatible with the vision of the program. These individuals will be much more likely to stay committed to the program over the course of time, and they are also more likely to put in the time and effort needed to implement the offense.

The formulation of a quality game plan really starts in the off-season each year. Many offensive staffs find it helpful to travel to both high schools and colleges each off-season and clinic with other staffs in order to gain greater insight into their own offense as well as what other programs are doing with their offenses. The willingness to share, change, and collaborate means that a staff can gain new insights into how to approach everything from game day organization of coaches, to play calling, to no-huddle structures. These off-season collaborations are the first key to creating a sound game plan system because they allow a staff to see what others are doing and adapt what they offer into a program.

Weekends

At the high school level, game plans are usually built in staff meeting rooms on weekends. The typical high school team plays their game around 7:00 p.m. on Friday night, and so most of the work for the next week must be accomplished on Saturday and Sunday. Following is one example of a game planning system that might be employed; it will be used as the model for how to game plan the air raid offense.

The game planning starts on Friday night after the game has finished. Once the players have left, the offensive coordinator takes the game film from the completed contest and loads it onto Hudl® to begin publishing to the Internet. While that film is burning, the offensive coordinator will also compile statistics for the game that was just finished (Figure 11-1). These statistics are critical in determining the course of the contest. These statistics are broken down into usable data that can be examined by the entire staff to determine strengths and weaknesses and the overall effectiveness of the game plan from the week before. A greater discussion of those stats will be discussed in a later portion of this chapter. When the coaching staff then meets on Saturday morning, the statistics from the night before as well as the film from that game are readily accessible. The next order of business will be a review of the team that will be faced the following week. The coverages, fronts, and stunts that the team uses are analyzed. Very few teams run the air raid offense, so it will not do much good to review how an opponent defended the team from the week before because many teams change their system to play an air raid offense. The basics will be outlined, and a game plan will be created based upon what the offense is designed to do. Most of the emphasis will be placed upon what the offense's athletes do well and not what the defense does structurally. The one exception is coverage. The coverage structure that the defense prefers might affect a few play calls, but generally fronts and blitzes do not necessitate much of a change to the game plan.

Use of Statistics to Build a Game Plan

Statistics, specifically the offense's own statistics, should be utilized to formulate a game plan. The majority of the game planning time is spent reviewing what the offense does well or what situations it most often finds itself in and not what the defense is attempting to do. Defenses are unpredictable, and there is no real way of knowing what they might do. Instead, it is generally more helpful to review your team's own offensive tendencies and positions in order to formulate what sort of attack might work. This chapter will use Nation Ford High School's 2012 season to illustrate how statistics are used to game plan the air raid offense.

Field position is the first indicator to review when determining a game plan. The field is divided into the goal line (or zero) out to the 20-yard line, the 21-yard line out to the 50-yard line, the 50-yard line down to the opponent's 21-yard line, the red zone from the opponent's 20-yard line down to the three-yard line, and a goal line zone from the

Game Stats vs. Opponent

Instructions: Fill in the player numbers and check off the box(es) for each run and pass play during the game.

Running Game

Player #	1	2	3	4	5	6	7	8	9	10	11	12	13

Passing Game

QB #	1	2	3	4	5	6	7	8	9	10	11	12	13
	14	15	16	17	18	19	20	21	22	23	24	25	26

Receiving Game

Player #	1	2	3	4	5	6	7	8	9	10	11	12	13

Fumbles: _____ Fumbles Lost: _____ Interceptions: _____

First Downs: _____ Points: _____ Time of Possession: _____

Total Yards: _____

Figure 11-1. Statistical chart

three-yard line to the opponent's end zone. Each of these sections then has a specific strategy for the offense. The goal of the offense is to throw the ball at least 60 percent of the time until they reach the 50-yard line, and then at least 50 percent of the time until they reach the goal line, at which point the passing goal should drop to about 40 percent. These figures are approximate, but the game planning goal is to put extensive pressure on the defense with the passing game while the offense has the most field to work with, which is from the offense's own goal line out to midfield. Once the midfield line is crossed, the offense can balance up between run and pass because the field is beginning to shorten, and so the running game will likely be more of a factor. However, if the offense continues passing at a rate over 60 percent all the way down the field, this is acceptable, but the number should not drop below 60 percent on the offense's own side of the field or 50 percent when on the defense's side of the field. These numbers were very well maintained except in the red zone (Figure 11-2). The red zone caused the play calling to become slightly more conservative than was expected, and this may have led to a slight drop in points for some games. This indicator by field position can be monitored throughout the game to gauge if the offense is being called properly and should be recorded after each contest.

Yard Line	Run Plays	Pass Plays
0 to 20	32%	65%
21 to 50	37%	62%
50 to 21	45%	55%
Red zone	56%	36%
Goal line	24%	47%

Figure 11-2. Field position chart

The next statistical indicator that is reviewed is the percentage of plays run by downs. Many teams will spend an extensive period of time working on third down, but in the air raid offense very little emphasis is placed on this down. The reason for this is that the majority of the plays called in a high school game are often first down calls (Figure 11-3). The simple fact that 76 percent of all play calls in 2012 were on first and second downs leads to the obvious conclusion that the play calls made on those two downs are of much more significance than third down calls. This information then should cause an analysis of the play calling distribution by down. Air raid teams must pass the football to be successful and, therefore, passing is the order of the day. The data clearly shows that a larger percentage of plays will be called on the first two downs of a series than on third down. Obviously, there will be a high rate of passing on third down, but it is necessary to also throw a great deal on first and second downs to keep the chains moving and stay out of third down situations. The goal will then be for the offense to throw the ball over 50 percent of the time on both first and second downs and over 60 percent of the time on third down. Fourth down is a statistical rarity, so those statistics do not enter into the game plan. In 2012, these numbers were achieved to the offense's credit (Figure 11-4).

Down	Percentage
First	47%
Second	29%
Third	19%
Fourth	4%

Figure 11-3. Down chart

Down	Run	Pass
First	48%	52%
Second	45%	55%
Third	34%	66%
Fourth	57%	43%

Figure 11-4. Play calling by downs chart

The next consideration is what formation the offense will line up in and how often for that particular opponent. The goal of the air raid offense in terms of formations is to use as many as possible without reducing speed. The offense is designed to be very fast-paced and to stress the defense. Therefore, it is necessary to keep the offense in a base structure of 2x2, 3x1 (regular or bunch), 3x2, or 4x1 for at least 60 percent of the game. These formations are all similar and require no substitutions, and so they allow the offense to move at a fast pace. The team spent a total of 69 percent of its time in those formations (Figure 11-5). There will be a need for other formations in order to attack specific defenses. These formations need to be decided upon, and there must also be a consensus of what plays will be run from these other formations that week so that teaching time is kept to a minimum. An example might be a two-back structure that gives the offense more of a power look. If this formation is deemed to be the most practical for a given opponent, then the entire staff will review it and make sure that the

Formation	Frequency of Use
2x2	32%
3x1	20%
I	10%
3x2	7%
Pistol	7%
Bunch	6%
4x1	4%
Two-tight-end	3%
Other	11%

Figure 11-5. Formations chart

exact run and pass plays to be utilized from that set are clear and a common theme of teaching is established.

The air raid offense's pass-oriented nature requires an analysis of pass zones to also be a major game planning priority. The field is broken up into six segments (Figure 11-6). The bottom three are from zero to six yards, the middle three are from 6 to 12 yards, and the top three are from 12 yards to the end zone. Zones 1 and 3 correspond to the flat, zone 2 is over the ball between the tackles, zones 4 and 6 are the sidelines to the hash marks, zone 5 is the intermediate middle of the field between the hash marks, zones 6 and 9 are the deep sidelines to the hash marks, and zone 8 is the deep middle of the field between the hash marks. These zones allow the offensive staff to

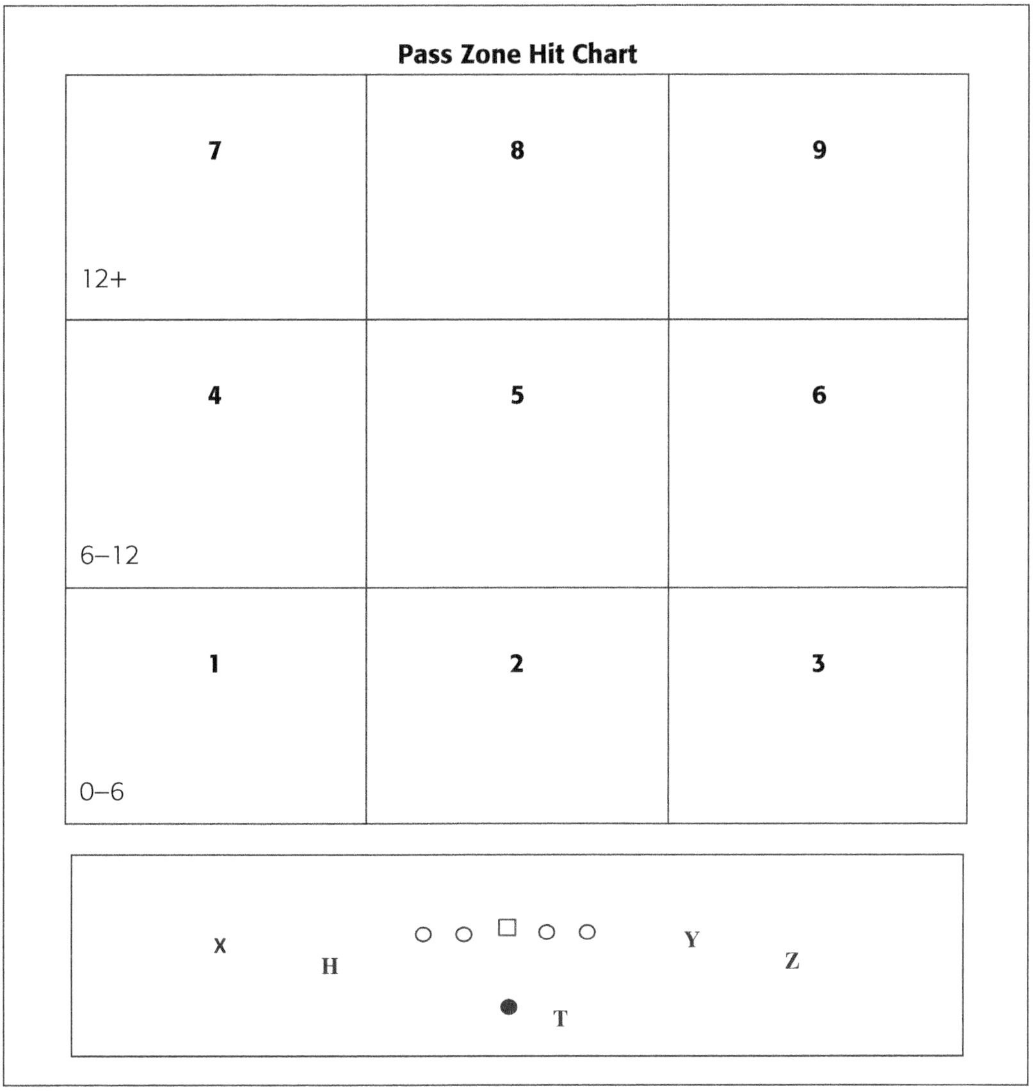

Pass Zone Hit Chart

12+	7	8	9
6–12	4	5	6
0–6	1	2	3

Figure 11-6. Field breakdown chart

determine where the ball is being thrown in order to determine if the offense can be easily prepared for by a defense. The offensive staff should strive to make sure there is a fair amount of balance between these zones so that opposing defense are unable to identify a zone that they need not defend. The offense did a great job of balancing the number of times each zone was thrown to during the season (Figure 11-7). The chart clearly shows that zones 1 and 3 were equal to one another, showing the offense threw to each flat an equal percentage of the time. In addition, zones 4 and 6 matched, and so did zones 7 and 9. This kind of offense play calling balance allows the play caller to see that he is using the entire field and forcing the defense to defend the entire width and depth of the field. This strategy of forcing defense to defend the entire field is a basic game plan of the air raid offense. If these numbers were to be out of balance, then the offensive staff would have to game plan ways to make sure that each zone was attacked equally in the next week. This balance keeps defenses from being able to accurately prepare for the offense by leaving some zones less defended and focusing on the offense's tendencies.

12+ yards	7 (7%)	8 (16%)	9 (7%)
6–12 yards	4 (6%)	5 (10%)	6 (6%)
0–6 yards	1 (20%)	2 (8%)	3 (20%)

Figure 11-7. Passing attack chart by field zone

Explosive Plays

In the air raid offense, it is necessary to create explosive plays. Explosive plays are defined as any play that gains 10 yards or more. Many factors can influence game planning, but this statistic helps to guide the thinking of many coaches. The philosophy in the air raid is that if the offense can generate explosive plays, the field position battle is constantly being won, but more importantly the offense is likely scoring a great deal of points. The goal was to score 30 points per game and so these explosive plays were needed in order to generate those sorts of point totals. If one of the major game planning goals of the offense is to create explosive plays, then it must be understood that there is a great deal of risk taking involved in the play calling, and there will also be negative plays. A total of 24 percent of all play calls resulted in an explosive play (Figure 11-8). There were a large number of negative or, more specifically, no-gain plays in the offense as well. Each time there is an incompletion, that adds to the number of no gain plays. Many coaches are not excited about having so many plays result in no gain, but even the National Football League has begun tracking explosive plays and minimizing

Result	Percentage
No gain (loss or incompletion)	37%
Small gain (1 to 3 yards)	15%
Medium gain (4 to 9 yards)	24%
Explosive gain (10+ yards)	24%

Figure 11-8. Result of plays chart

the detriment of no-gain types of plays. The team had 126 plays that gained 10 yards or more, and these 126 plays generated over 2,000 yards of total offense. This kind of risk/reward is not only acceptable, but it is part of the overall strategy of a good air raid offense. The risks of a few no-gain plays are far outweighed by the fact that the offense produced over 2,000 yards in only 126 snaps of offense.

The idea of creating explosive plays is a guiding factor in how coaches should construct their offensive game plan. Further reflection shows that the majority of the explosive plays came from the forward pass, as might be expected in the air raid offense (Figure 11-9). The offensive staff then broke down where those pass plays were thrown using an explosive hit chart for the pass plays that utilized the same passing zones table that was used to determine where the ball was thrown (Figure 11-10). Analysis of this chart shows that the offense is generating an equal distribution of explosive plays all over the field. This chart shows that the coaching staff is, in fact, calling plays and teaching concepts to get the ball into playmakers hands all over the football field.

The final aspect of explosive plays guiding the game plan is to make sure that the plays that lead to explosive yardage are being called each week. This is accomplished by reviewing which plays actually result in an explosive amount of yardage

Type of Play	Percentage of Explosive Plays
Run	28%
Pass	72%

Figure 11-9. Explosive play-by-play call chart

12+ yards	7 (35%)	8 (42%)	9 (13%)
6–12 yards	4 (47%)	5 (37%)	6 (59%)
0–6 yards	1 (20%)	2 (19%)	3 (31%)

Figure 11-10. Explosive play-by-pass zone chart

(Figure 11-11). The chart allows the staff to see (in this instance, for a whole season) which plays were safe to call in order to create an explosive amount of yardage. It is then the responsibility of the coaching staff to ensure that these plays are called as often as possible. During the season, the school averaged 10.5 explosive plays per game. This average was maintained because the staff constantly called plays in each game that came from the statistical charts of most explosive plays. This gives the play caller a sounder basis for making his calls and roots the play calling in scientific facts that can be analyzed after each contest.

Play Name	Play Type	Percentage of Explosive Plays
Texas Tech Z Comeback	Pass	100%
Texas Tech X Comeback	Pass	75%
Arizona Pound	Run	50%
Texas Tech	Pass	45%
Houston	Pass	31%
Ducks 3	Screen	29%
Florida	Pass	27%
Texas Tech Switch	Pass	25%
Jersey	Run	23%
Giants	Run	22%
Arizona/Pittsburgh	Run	13%

Figure 11-11. Plays that resulted in explosive yardage chart

Coach Responsibilities on Game Night

The final piece of the game plan is the actual calling of plays. This is best accomplished by one coach so that the play calls are sent in quickly and with minimal distraction. It is both possible and preferable for coaches to meet in between series to collaborate on the play calling and what might be possible to run, but this should not be done during a series.

The play caller, usually the offensive coordinator, should stand behind the defense, and he is responsible for communicating the play, direction, and formation through his headset to the two signaling coaches. The two signaling coaches, usually the inside and outside receivers' coaches, will be responsible for the hand signals that get the formation, direction, and play call to the players on the field. One of these coaches will be "live," meaning his call is what the players are looking at, and the other will be "dead," meaning that his signal is a decoy. While this is being done, the offensive line coach will be watching defensive techniques and stunts by the defensive line and linebackers. This coach will make adjustments to the offensive line as needed. The running backs coach will assist the offensive coordinator in watching coverage and any other situations that might arise on the sideline. This collaborative effort is essential for success when running an up-tempo offense. Communication is mainly flowing out from the play caller, and very little information is returning via the signaling coaches or other staff members. The collaborative nature of the staff plays out in between series when the staff meets together and with the team to work on issues before the next series.

Execution of the Game Plan

The game plan for a Friday night game would have been formulated the Saturday before in staff meetings. At that time, the offensive staff would have decided what sort of pass and run plays would most effectively attack the defense that week. In addition, emphasis would have been placed on which plays calls were most likely to produce explosive plays that week. The offensive staff would have reviewed all formations, tags, and other adjustments for that week that would have given the team the greatest likelihood of success. These plays would then be practiced throughout the week and reviewed on Thursday night one final time in preparation for the Friday night contest.

The game plan in the air raid offense is commonly not written down. The game plan is not a new structure every week but a slight alteration from one week to the next of the basic offensive package. Therefore, the entire team knows the plays, tags, and formations already and is simply reviewing throughout the week the actual concepts that are most likely to lead to offensive production. The final game plan is then reviewed with the quarterbacks and coaches one last time over team dinner on Friday afternoon. This plan is simply verbalized. In fact, it is preferable to not even have written copies of the plan to distribute to coaches. It has been formulated that individuals are more likely to buy into a plan that is simple and easy to remember. Therefore, the game plan never changes much from week to week to keep it simple and easy to remember. This game plan is called and executed from the outset of the game. Oftentimes, it is more of a guideline than a set of rules to govern the play calling. Many defenses attempt unconventional responses to playing an air raid offense. These responses vary from playing a typical base coverage to utilizing a completely new coverage that has never been seen on film. It is necessary, then, as a play caller, to prepare for what the coach has seen on film, but to keep the offensive game plan simple and flexible enough to evolve as the game progresses.

Conclusion

Many teams feel that scripting plays or producing dozens of pages of documentation for a game plan is a good way to prepare for a contest. This is certainly possible to do and works for many coaches. However, the air raid offense is so dynamic and different from what most coaches see from week to week that it causes defenses to respond in unpredictable fashions. Instead of the formulating a game plan that is overly detailed, it is preferable to identify what type of defense the opponent plays and formulate a simple and flexible response.

The idea of a flexible response means that the offense should prepare base sets of concepts that attack any coverage and have tags available to all those plays to attack what the defense might do to adjust. This strategy removes the need for complex game plan forms. Instead, the offense decides what concepts will work best versus an opponent, practices several countermeasures for what the defense might do, and then proceeds to the contest with confidence that a variety of solutions are available to any problem. This style of game planning is less conventional than that of many teams, but it allows the offense to focus its time more on practicing and watching film to discover techniques of defenders rather than preparing elaborate game planning forms that might not be utilized on Friday nights. Game planning is a collaborative effort and includes the coaches as well as the athletes. It should be remembered, however, that the best game plans are usually those that are simple and easy to teach throughout the week, but are still flexible enough to respond to any eventuality on game nights.

Conclusion

The game of football is certainly a cyclical process to say the least. The Houston veer, the Delaware wing-T, the Oklahoma wishbone, they have all come and, by and large, gone. These systems left indelible marks on the game of football and gave it some substantial foundation to build and grow from for the future. The air raid offense takes its place beside these great offenses in the pantheon of football greatness, but unlike these systems, it has endured for a very simple reason: it is versatile. The air raid is not an offense that requires adherence to specific sets of rules in order to claim a place in its fraternity. In fact, the unconventional "adjust to fit the talent" mind-set of the air raid and other spread offense today is exactly why it might be said that we have entered a prolonged period of football history known as the era of the spread.

The air raid offense and it spread offense and zone read offense cousins are always changing and ever fluid in their styles. When looking at University of West Virginia, East Carolina University, Texas Tech University, Baylor University, Oklahoma State University, Murray State University, Louisiana Tech University, and others, you see a wide range of teams that either call themselves air raid offense or take very heavy doses of the system and tweak it to fit their personnel. There is no guarantee that a 6'5" strong-armed quarterback will be on the team each year any more than there are consistent odds of a 220-pound tailback being on that team. The simple truth is that sports are dynamic endeavors that require a great deal of flexibility in order for the system and the program running a particular system to survive. The air raid lends itself to this fluid landscape of modern sports quite well. A wide range of quarterback types from athletes such as Graham Harrell and Brandon Weeden to Robert Griffin III and Geno Smith have made names and fortunes for themselves playing in air raid systems that alter the nature of the offense to accentuate their specific talents. This is done at every position on the field, including the receiver position, where athletes as diverse as Justin Blackmon and Wes Welker have found homes and illustrious receiving totals because of the flexibility in the air raid offense of getting them the ball. This is true of every position on the field.

The air raid offense defies the conventional wisdom of gaining first downs, controlling blocks, and winning field position, and it reduces offensive goals to the main priority of scoring enough points to outscore opponents. That is what offensive football is really designed to do, and the air raid allows coaches to do it in whatever manner they choose. If the athletic potential in a given year means that the run game is emphasized or the quick passing game needs to be a priority, then those things can be easily accomplished. This offense allows a coach to wring optimum rewards out of athletes despite limited physical dominance. A quick glance at the collegiate career of Case Keenum or the still-unfinished career of Heisman Trophy winner Johnny Manziel will provide evidence of two athletes who were regarded as not big enough or not strong enough to play at other institutions, but went on to score points, smash records, and deliver wins at air raid–inspired schools.

The air raid offense is a viable and integral part of the football landscape for the foreseeable future because it allows teams to be flexible as well as aggressive in designing their systems. This system allows coaches to put their players in position to succeed while taking risks and attacking defenses. The air raid offense is a fun system to coach and play in, and so it lends itself well to the nature of prep and collegiate sports. These levels of sports are facing increasing pressure from other sports and activities for athletes' time and focus. When the game of football if played at a fast pace and multiple athletes are allowed to touch the ball and sport points, then the game is made more fun to participate in and watch. These factors help coaches to attract the best athletes to the football field, where they can showcase their talents. This showcase has been well documented for decades and will continue to flourish well into the 21st century.

About the Author

Rich Hargitt has been coaching since 1999. He has served as a head football coach and offensive coordinator at the high school level in Illinois, Indiana, North Carolina, and South Carolina. He is currently the passing game coordinator/receivers coach at Ashbrook High School in North Carolina.

Hargitt's teams have utilized the air raid offense to upset several ranked teams and the offense has produced school record holders in rushing and passing. Hargitt's first air raid quarterback, Mitch Niekamp, holds several college records at Illinois College and is a starting quarterback in Europe's professional leagues. In 2011, Hargitt took the air raid offense to Nation Ford High School, where he helped lead the Falcons to their first non-losing season, first AAA region victory, first AAA playoff berth, and first AAA playoff victory. In 2012, Hargitt's offense broke the school single-game and single-season offensive records for passing yards, touchdowns, and points scored, and he helped guide the Falcons to a AAAA playoff berth for the first time in school history.

Hargitt contributed to a six-part video series on the spread wing-T offense for *American Football Monthly* and has been published numerous times in coaching journals on the air raid offense. He has spoken about the air raid offense at both the Nike Coach of the Year Clinics and the Glazier Clinics. He is also the author of *101 Shotgun Wing-T Plays* (cowritten with Lew Johnston) and *101 Air Raid Plays*, and is the featured speaker on a series of DVDs detailing the air raid offense.

In 2010, he earned a master's of arts degree in physical education with coaching specialization from Ball State University. Hargitt resides in Gastonia, North Carolina, with his wife, Lisa, and their sons, Griffin and Graham.